WAYWARD

WAYWARD

Just Another Life to Live

Vashti Bunyan

**WHITE
RABBIT**

First published in Great Britain in 2022 by White Rabbit,
an imprint of The Orion Publishing Group Ltd
Carmelite House, 50 Victoria Embankment
London EC4Y 0DZ

An Hachette UK Company

1 3 5 7 9 10 8 6 4 2

A CIP catalogue record for this book is
available from the British Library.

ISBN (Hardback) 978 1 4746 2193 9
ISBN (eBook) 978 1 4746 2196 0
ISBN (Audio) 978 1 4746 2197 7

Printed in Great Britain by Clays Ltd, St Ives plc

www.whiterabbitbooks.co.uk
www.orionbooks.co.uk

For all who have left and for all who have stayed

Helen Edith Bunyan

Beginnings

My name is Jennifer Vashti Bunyan, but I have never been known as Jennifer. In the Book of Esther, Old Testament, Vashti is the wife of King Ahasuerus and is banished for refusing to dance for his guests at a banquet. It was my grandfather's nickname for my mother Helen, his future daughter-in-law. He meant she was awkward and stubborn, but I like to remember it as the dark-eyed rebellion of a spirited young woman.

Later my father had a boat he named the *Vashti*, and when I came along in 1945 (ten years after my brother John and five years after my sister Susan Jane), I am told that I was named after the boat. My paternal grandmother thought that I should be Jennifer first, a proper name, she said, though even she never called me that.

My mother lost a child before me, and one after me, both boys; and so maybe I was a bit of a disappointment. She was apparently very ill after my birth so I was handed over to her mother for my first days. I was never fond of that grandmother. She was a rather cold and distant person, not very motherly. I later learned that she had been orphaned and sent into service when very young, eventually to be a companion to a French woman who seldom got out of her bed, wore her best hat in it and who insisted on the silver tea set at every teatime. I believe this was where my grandmother learned her airs and graces, and the disapproval she showed off so well with her up-tilted chin.

I understand the way she was now, since finding out that as an officer's wife, she'd had to keep well hidden that her father – my mother's grandfather – was a Romany Traveller.

In recent years I have been told of this deeply buried family secret – never mentioned when there was ever a question of how it was that my mother had such raven-black hair in her family of fair siblings. I wish that Grandma had been able to tell me. Or even her son, my Uncle William, when I was visiting him as a child. He used to slow down as we drove past the brightly painted horse-drawn wagons and the wildly different-looking people with their defiant stares, parked up on the verges of the Kentish roads. I would have liked to know – as he must have done – that we were maybe related to them, even distantly.

Oak House

My family moved when I was six months old from Newcastle upon Tyne, where I was born, to Oak House, number 5 Wildwood Rise, London, NW11, just by the Hampstead Heath Extension and built in about 1914. Oak panelling, parquet floors, golden-oak staircase surrounding the hall with a window seat halfway up, a large grassy garden mown to perfection and hollyhocks either side of the big arched front door. There was a cook in the kitchen and from time to time a nanny to look after me. My older sister didn't seem to need much looking after as she spent all her time reading, or being tortured by my very existence.

I was about three when, one night, our mother, rather than the nanny, had been the one to give us our bedtime bath, sitting us both down afterwards by the nursery fire. She combed my sister's straight blond hair, and scraped two kirby grips into each side of her middle parting, put her in her bed with a book, and then spent long minutes happily cutting up rags to make curlers for my wavy brown hair so that the next day I would have lovely ringlets.

Leaving us to go downstairs to get us some supper, she must have been gone a while, for when she returned Susan Jane was still sitting in her bed, still reading but with narrowed eyes, and little Vashti was sitting bolt upright and saucer-eyed in hers, surrounded by rags, curls, *eyelashes* – and scissors. I have checked the truth of this story recently, asking if I'd maybe made up the bit about the eyelashes?

My sister says, 'No, no, I did do it.' I wonder how she got me to keep still.

There was an orange in segments on the supper tray, a rare post-war treat. Our mother said nothing but I was quietly given every bit of it. Sister Sue insisted she didn't like oranges anyway, not wanting anyone to think she cared. I love my sister.

A while later I was looking up at her, adoringly, through my fever of 105°F with pneumonia, as she fiercely read to me whilst we waited for the ambulance. She was probably hoping I would not die even if she had so wished me to just vanish, sometimes. Often.

I lived, after two weeks on my own in a hospital room, saved by the penicillin jammed into my backside four times a day with a nurse on each limb holding me down. Visitors were allowed once a week, maybe to check that I was still alive.

Susan and Vashti

* * *

My father had a large collection of 78rpm classical records. Every Sunday the house would be filled with music and he would stand at the top of the stairs, conducting his ghostly orchestra down in the hall. My earliest musical memory was my love for Beethoven's Pastoral Symphony, but just a small part of it – the final few minutes. I ruined my father's record of this by playing the last lilting strings and birdsong over and over, completely uncaring of the wrath I'd incur. They took the needle out of the gramophone. I got a sewing needle, turned on the turntable and could hear just enough to keep me happy. The damage was of course even worse, 78s being made of shellac and very fragile, so when I hear it now I am small again and getting yelled at. It was worth it, as I remember.

I also remember wanting to be a boy – but only partly because I wanted to be the choirboy who sang 'O, for the wings, for the wings of a dove'.

My brother John was ten years older and my earliest memories of him are of the delicate balsa-wood planes he made in the attic, and his disembodied grin like the Cheshire cat in *Alice in Wonderland*. At fifteen years old he was sent to a school in the United States on an exchange for a year – to our mother's great distress, missing her boy, her precious son. He came back with a suitcase full of all that was needed to make a player for the new 33rpm long-playing records, all the wiring and valves, switches and Bakelite knobs, along with LPs of my father's favourite Bach and Beethoven. I was allowed to watch with wonder as everything was strewn across the usually pristine sitting room, with a piece of plywood sawn up for a turntable making a glorious sawdusty mess. Sundays would now be louder than ever.

So, for some peace, Mum would go over the road to number 3, Appletree Wick, where her famous actress friend Roma Beaumont lived with her husband, the impresario Alfred Black. Their house was different. White, always warm, lit by many silk-shaded lamps on gilded tables, with soft pale fitted carpets, a high-sided velvet sofa with tassels at each corner – and a faint scent of gin in amongst the roses.

They had a Rolls-Royce and their occasional lifts into the city made me sick with the swooping and the new leather – my father's cars being more of the vintage type and usually leaking and draughty. The damp upholstery and old, overheated oil never troubled me.

———

London, W1

In 1951, when I was six, Dad had a heart attack. He was so ill that he was told he must not work for a while, nor drive, or do anything much at all for the rest of his life in case it were to happen again.

The Hotchkiss, and Oak House

Oak House had to be sold, also his beloved 1930s Hotchkiss convertible, and I watched as my own beloved big black grand piano was sawn up since no one in those post war-torn days would want it. Even the dog was given away. My mother's life changed for what must have seemed like the very worst as we all had to move, away from her very close friends and theatrical neighbours, into the top two dilapidated floors of the house in central London where my father had his dental surgery and laboratory.

22 Seymour Street, London, W1, had survived the wartime bombing although there was an impressive dent in the wall at the back of the hall where the front door had landed after a blast from a near miss.

It was a tall, thin, Georgian brick house of six floors, on

the corner of a long terrace. Dark, narrow staircases were painted gloomy green and brown, with green and brown worn lino on every stair and every floor. There was a crack in my bedroom wall through which sunlight, moonlight and streetlamps shone. No cook, no nanny. The room we lived in at the top of the house had a two-ring Belling cooker on a tin-topped table, a clothes pulley hanging from the ceiling and a big china sink with a wooden draining board. Mum shed many tears into that sink, and now even more often than before (and there had been many times) I would find her furiously weeping into a half-packed suitcase – 'I'm going back to my mother.' She never did.

After a while the tenant who occupied the middle floor was asked to leave and so we had an actual kitchen and a sitting room, which made things a lot better for my dear brave mum. There was now a place for her spindly little Edwardian mahogany desk, where she did her sums and tried to make sense of my father's spending. It was slightly shaky and it is a treasured memory – the sound of the ice tinkling in her gin and tonic and the jingle of her silver bracelets as she added up her long columns of figures.

Wilder Child

There's something to be said for being the youngest, as I was now given a lot of freedom. It was probably hard to keep me in since I had been so used to roaming wherever I wanted when we lived by Hampstead Heath. Here in the middle of London I played with the children from the streets nearby, on the bombsites that surrounded us. I read BEWARE FALLING MASONRY in big red letters, but it meant nothing to us as we scrambled over the bricks and stones and blackened, broken rafters – looking for signs of the people who must have lived there, hoping to find bones.

Coming home one day I ran past the door where my father was bowing and shepherding out a patient, a large perfumed woman in an even larger brown fur coat, tiny shoes and a jaunty hat. He was kissing her hand goodbye. He spied me with dismay, his small daughter, with one long plait undone and the ribbon lost, one sock up, one down, muddy knees and happy face saying hello. He waved me away up the rest of the stairs to the top of the house where I stayed, content to be by myself in the room with my goldfish, the sink, and the boiler which rumbled and shook in its cupboard.

The room next to my father's surgery was his laboratory, and resembled the set of a 1950s horror movie. All sizes of test tubes, bottles with yellowed and peeling labels, body bits pickled in jars, an untidy dark-yellow and incomplete skeleton and a shabby cardboard box containing human ribs, a skull and a thigh bone. Dentistry bored him; he spent as little time as possible being one and preferred to spend his days experimenting and inventing – 'innovating' as he called it. No one was allowed in to clean and so the dust lay – but never seemed to get any worse. An early lesson in housekeeping for me.

Sometimes he remembered I was there and took me into his lab to teach me about electricity and the internal combustion engine. Then there was the frog. How he got a hold of a live one I do not know, but he knocked it out with a needle in the back of its little green head, 'pithing' he called it. He pinned it out by its legs and arms, crucified on its back on a wooden board, and, since it was unconscious (he said) but still alive – he cut it open to show me its tiny heart beating. This was to teach me about circulation and the nervous system. I have a hazy memory of later finding it withered up in the dust and taking it away to bury it in the gardens at the end of our street. I might be making the burial bit up, but the rest is clear as day.

After we'd moved into central London our erstwhile neighbours the Blacks from Appletree Wick would visit regularly, my mother would have her hair done in anticipation – and I would be cleaned up. An unannounced visit had me being dragged into the bathroom and Chanel No. 5 poured onto the top of my head to drown out the wild child. I tried to wriggle out of my mother's determined grasp but had to suffer the rest of the day in a cloud of the stuff.

Lessons

I wanted to go to the same school as my friends who lived nearby but after managing to fail the entrance exam, and then passing the next year, I was eventually sent to Queen's College, Harley Street. My sister had gone there before me and was a spectacular student where I was not. I did make one very good friend there though, and at weekends I would get a bus out to her and her mother's house. I did not know their story but she had no father. We got into big trouble for breaking a window in the school and my parents and her mother were called in, so from then on we were forbidden to play together or visit each other's homes. I was told later that she was the illegitimate daughter of a man who had paid for her school fees, and that my parents had been told this was the reason I had become such a hooligan. One accidentally broken window. We were eleven, maybe twelve, and we missed each other.

Just another lesson to add to the one I'd had at four years old when my only friend was the son of the cook next door. We were found one day in the garage where we had not noticed that there was a window through which we could be seen taking all our clothes off – both curious to discover our differences. He was blamed for leading me astray, because he was the son of a cook, and had no visible father. Banished. I really missed him.

Education

By 1958, my brother had gone away, married and had a baby, my beautiful, elegant, debutante sister had eloped off to New York – and I wanted to be Davy Crockett.

When found sobbing in a wardrobe at thirteen years old I said it was because I missed my brother and sister. I lied. It was really because I had just discovered that Fess Parker, the film actor who played Davy Crockett, lived on the other side of the world. The nurse who looked after the dental practice – a thankless task, a kind woman only referred to as 'Nurse', I never knew her name – had gently told me that looking for F. Parker in the London telephone directory down in the office would not find him as he actually lived a *million* miles away.

I feigned many ways to be too ill to go to school that year, thin, pale, listless, eventually getting measles and oh, the triumph of having a real illness with spots. At fourteen it was decided to send me away – out of London and into the country air. My father had a pathologist friend whose daughter had just run away from a school in deepest Kent and so there was a place for me.

Lillesden School for Girls, Hawkhurst, January 1959. Ugly, Victorian Gothic, red brick, with turrets and freezing dormitories. My hooligan reputation had gone before me and I was put in the not-too-clever class. The first morning at assembly I was presented to the school as the new girl and when my name was announced the laughs went around the room and came back to me with a rush of heat to my face. I cried for days, a puzzle to the other children who had mostly been there since the age of eight and seemingly preferred school to home. My heart was with the one who had run away.

It was the kind of education I don't think my parents

had in mind. Our letters home were censored and so my closed world became just these girls and extraordinary, mixed-together women – women who were in some cases bitter and cruel, in others inspiring and kind. The kindest I remember was a music teacher with a tattooed number on her forearm which she showed us often, but without any stories to go with it we just had to guess.

Most memorable was Matron, who ran the school clinic with a rod of iron – and a daily dose of syrup of figs. Terrifying, she was stout, with short, sharp bristly hair, and she stamped around on her Jacobean table-like legs, dressed in full nurse uniform, getting as many people into trouble as she could – with trumped-up charges. Every Friday she and the local doctor would have all the sickly ones lined up and whatever was wrong with anyone always required complete undressing – whether sore ankle or sore throat. Matron was apparently asked to leave, along with another teacher, when they were found in the back of the laundry room with one in her underwear. This would have gone quite unnoticed, or even remarked upon as odd, had the child who witnessed it not described the scene to a visiting parent who was shocked. The innocence of parents.

My violin came with me. I'd found it in Portobello Road Market and my brother had given me the two pounds that I needed to buy it. The music teacher at my day school told me to ask my parents to insure it well as it was really very good, she said.

The violin teacher at my 'expensive orphanage'* was a spectral figure in a long black gown, with perfectly white hair curled under the back of her tiny neck and a black velvet ribbon around her forehead. I never saw her feet as she went gliding her way around the school and we barely spoke but I was drawn to her quiet, distant ways. However, she did have me play 'Twinkle, Twinkle, Little Star' every week for the whole term, so I left the violin at home for my second term. I never saw it again as my father sold it for a tenner to someone who came to the door looking for old things.

Oh Boy!

Throughout the years there had been regular visits back to our old theatrical neighbours the Blacks at Appletree Wick. The peace and order of that house was in such contrast to mine, with its sunlit garden and blond, carefree children.

During one much later visit in 1958 I saw Jack Good's TV show *Oh Boy!* for the first time. The first UK pop-music programme. Billy Fury, Marty Wilde, Cliff Richard and the Shadows. We had no TV – but the Blacks of course did.

* quoting Andrew Loog Oldham.

Alfred Black and his brother George promoted summer shows at the Blackpool Opera House. Venues such as this – ballrooms, dance halls and theatres across the land – were more or less the only places to see live popular music at this time, slowly taking over from music hall. In 1961 the headliner was Cliff Richard and after much pleading my mother agreed to take me to see the show and afterwards to go backstage with Alfred to get an autographed photograph.

Accommodation that summer in Blackpool was hard to find. My mother and I shared a creaky bed in the attic of a boarding house – but I didn't care about her discomfort, blinded as I was by the thought of seeing someone real and alive on the stage and not just on the Blacks' black and white TV.

He sang with the Shadows, shining into my sixteen-year-old mind and I was incandescent until . . . we were shown into a drab and smoky dressing room full of *old* people who were talking loudly, drinking, laughing, and where he stood, still, silent, leaning back against a benchtop before a lightbulb-surrounded mirror. His arms were folded, his ankles crossed, and he was looking at me with large brown, almost black, eyes. Unsmiling, angry.

My bliss turned to sorrow; was he hating his life? Just twenty years old, a trapped deer, seemingly hating me. Even as young as I was, I felt bad for him. What must it be like to be him?

I had seen him in the film *Expresso Bongo* when I was fourteen – just before being disappeared off to boarding school to right my ways – and it had stayed with me.

The Soho sleaze, the lure of that place in London I was not allowed to go near, the hinted-at underworld of pop music, beguiling and drawing me towards it in ways I would not have had the words nor wit to understand.

Cliff Richard

Back to School

Those in the not-too-clever class were not allowed to take O levels. As awkward and shy as I was, I knocked on the head-mistress's door and asked permission to take them anyway. She was a very big woman in plain straight dresses that had split many times down their side seams and been stitched up again untidily, this being the main thing I really noticed about her – except that she was very stern. Never smiled. With her chin up she looked down at me forbiddingly and said, 'You won't let me down, will you?'

I didn't, and when I went back for my last year I was allowed the run of the art room. I have one A level. Art.

During that last school year, the confirmation service in the local church brought us a bishop to solemnly lay his hands on our heads, as we obediently knelt before him in our white dresses.

'Did you feel anything?'

'No.'

'Neither did I.'

* * *

My father had bought me a piano for passing my O levels, from the junk shop around the corner. He paid a tenner for it – *my* tenner I thought, for my violin. Golden walnut, inlaid all over with flowers and swags, with little brass candle holders. Out of tune, but my mother played it sometimes and sang softly in a beautiful voice as I watched her through a slightly open door, feeling sorrow for the life she must have given up to marry my father.

By the time I was home he had sold it to someone who came to the door looking for old things. Again.

What to Do with Her

Dad had a surgeon friend whose daughter had gone to the Ruskin School of Drawing and Fine Art in Oxford. There she had met and married the son of a Scottish lord.

I was sent to the Ruskin School of Drawing and Fine Art.

The art school was held in two lofty rooms in the Ashmolean Museum. As I arrived at the door of the museum, a blond-haired, strikingly beautiful girl had got there at the same time. I don't remember which one of us dropped our portfolio, spilling drawings all over the steps, but we both thought it was funny and so Jenny Lewis and I have been firm friends ever since.

No painting for the first year, only drawing the plaster casts of ancient Greek torsos, down in the basement.

My way of drawing had always been cartoon-like but this was frowned upon most fiercely. So, I was bored with the cast room and found much more to interest me in the museum itself. The Egyptian mummies, the sixteenth-century lutes with their intricate carving inside the sound holes, the Uccello hunting scene and the Pre-Raphaelite paintings seemingly just there to be laughed at. Also, Jenny found friends who would hugely affect our lives over the next years, the Experimental Theatre Company, Michael Palin and Terry Jones – the birth and early days of Monty Python.

I soon moved into a room next to Jenny, a tiny room on the attic floor of a terraced house in Iffley Road. Jenny had a guitar, and a book – Bert Weedon's *Play in a Day*. My violin lessons came in handy, and although I had never learned to read music (and still have not) I was able to pick up Jenny's guitar and quickly find my way.

My sister-in-law lent me her grandmother's guitar and so with Jenny in her room and me in mine, we each wrote songs – sweet simple songs which I still treasure.

My first song was 'I Don't Know What Love Is'. The last line was:

Want you to be with me and wonder why,
there never was a love for you and I

My father said, 'You and *ME*, you and *ME* – and after all I *spent* on your education.'

You and me didn't rhyme.

Jenny came home one night slightly drunk – I was impressed as she wove her way into my room. We sat on the floor with our guitars and started to laugh about seeing pink elephants, playing around with the different chords we were starting to find. Together we wrote 'Seventeen pink sugar elephants, sitting under a chestnut tree'. *Magic everywhere.*

Jenny got the part of the lion tamer in the Oxford University Dramatic Society production of Leonid Andreyev's play *He Who Gets Slapped*. How magnificent she was, cracking a whip with one hand whilst smoking a cigarette held in the other. I got the part of the maid who runs in from the wings at the end and cries 'The Baron has shot himself'. It came out – in my attempted Russian accent – as 'Zee baron has shat himself' and the explosive laugh from the back of the hall was, of course, my father. It ruined the tragedy of the scene and was the end of my stage career.

My godfather's daughter – Angy Strange – joined Jenny and me at the Ruskin. We sang together as The Three of Us, and somehow we landed a job at a charity ball in Grosvenor House, Park Lane. Dressed in Mary Quant we sang Everly Brothers and Buddy Holly songs in perfect harmony, and were approached afterwards by a man calling himself an entrepreneur – with the name Mervyn Conn. He offered us a contract and we all just said ha-ha – no. Of course, he became very successful, but I believe he is now in jail for historic offences against young women, and will be there for some time to come.

After two years of the Ruskin I was asked to leave. I had spent too much time with my guitar, in bed or painting scenery for the theatre company. Much time was also spent in the college room of an undergraduate called Robert Hewison, whilst he and Mike Palin and Terry Jones created and acted out their revue sketches and had me laughing until I thought I might die. Nothing has ever felt so painfully funny since those moments. I loved them with all my heart for the way they saw the world, and the way they had me see it with them.

The outgoing principal of the art school was a softly spoken, kind man and was inclined to let me stay for the third year, but he was being replaced by a much tougher character altogether. When I told him I thought art was art whatever the medium he said to go and do my art elsewhere; 'HERE YOU PAINT AND DRAW'.

Jenny and Angy continued to paint and draw, but later – as Jennifer Lewis and Angela Strange – they went on to record and release two singles on Columbia, beautiful songs written by Jenny.

New York

My sister was always the clever one with whom I was compared unfavourably – she was bound for great things according to our father. He had ambitions for his older daughter, unusual for his generation. However, at eighteen she met a newly qualified young houseman, a junior doctor, when having her appendix out. He came to sit on her hospital bed in the night and read poetry to her. I was twelve and loved the romance of it, but our father did not and sent her away to the USA where she was charged with looking after the British stand at an international trade fair in Texas. While there she discovered that in the USA a person could be married at eighteen without paternal permission whilst in Britain it was still twenty-one. They married in New York whilst Dad bellowed down the phone at the NY police to 'FIND MY DAUGHTER'. The NY Police Dept did not scour the New York City streets searching for a very young, very English woman who was defying her father, and so my sister and her new husband stayed in New York after being told that she had made her bed and must now lie in it. They have lived there ever since, Dad coming round eventually – after his son-in-law became a successful Park Avenue psychoanalyst.

*　*　*

What could anyone do with me after my being told to leave the Ruskin? (I used to be listed on the Ruskin's Wikipedia page as an alumna but I have been removed, no doubt because my own Wikipedia page tells of my expulsion.) At nineteen I was sent off to New York to help look after my sister's children, by now three of the four boys she would have. Being 'sent' was the way of things then. It seems ridiculous now, but then it was normal parenting.

Knowing I was bored and unhappy, my brother-in-law took me down to the East Village one day. If in 1964 I had been brave and free – and not so well protected in order to stop me getting into trouble – I might have sought out the musicians playing there at the time. My life could have taken a different course, but as it was, all I could find of them was *The Freewheelin' Bob Dylan* vinyl album staring at me from a record shop window.

In my last weeks in Oxford I had fallen for – and ridden behind – a lovely, guitar-playing, Norton 500 biker. He wore a red neckerchief, a leather jacket and he worshipped Bob Dylan. He played 'Blowin' in the Wind' endlessly and affectingly, but he would not teach it to me because he said a girl should not be singing a Dylan song. I'd left him way behind, but I bought the album in that East Village shop – and taught myself. The songs taught me a lot more, and led me into a world of which I knew little and so began to fill some of the air in my head.

I ran away from New York, deserted my courageous, homesick sister and her beautiful blond boys in matching everything, and went home to London full of ideas, songs and ambition to become a wandering troubadour with my guitar over my back, and nothing matching. The first song I heard on the radio when I was home was 'As Tears Go By' by Marianne Faithfull. I sat on my bed and wept – as well I might – as comparisons with her so haunted me over the years.

Compromise

My parents asked my big brother to give me a talking-to. What was I going to do with myself now? How will I make a living? Secretary? Nurse? Get *MARRIED*? Ugh.

'I want to be a pop singer.'

My brother laughed. His lovely big drain laugh that I so miss now he's gone, but then it just made me narrow my eyes.

Undaunted and determined I went up and down Denmark Street in Soho – London's Tin Pan Alley – looking for any managers or producers who might listen to me and my guitar. They had to shut their windows in order to hear me over the noise of the traffic outside and one patted me on the backside as he showed me the door, saying, 'Very nice but you're just not commercial, dear.'

Maybe he just couldn't imagine me in a sparkling ballgown with my hair lacquered up on top of my head. I couldn't either.

I borrowed some money and booked an hour in a studio where I recorded twelve songs straight, one after another, just voice and guitar, with my very English tones announcing each title as I went. I had four of the songs put onto a seven-inch acetate, and this was my only demo. I lost it. I wonder if anyone ever found it.

Looking for any opportunity to be heard, I took up the offer of a spot in a bar called the Dark Room. Girl with guitar singing quiet songs to fur-coated, loudly drunken and perfumed *old* people who must have been quite bewildered at the sight and sound of me. Not that they could hear me. One time only.

There was a party given by our old neighbours the Blacks at Appletree Wick, just before my twentieth birthday. My mother persuaded me to go with her and I reluctantly took my guitar and sat down on the edge of a gilt chair in a room full of once-famous actresses, singers, people of the stage. Mink coats, diamonds and pearls, patent leather shoes, gin and tonics, Mum happily back with friends. I chose to quietly sing 'How Do I Know', probably hoping to raise some perfect eyebrows with its reference to having babies by different fathers and still being free.

I remember making no impression amongst the clinking glasses and high laughter, but I must have done on one woman there – an agent called Monte Mackey from the Al Parker agency in Mayfair.

Mrs Mackey knew Andrew Loog Oldham – twenty-one-year-old manager of the Rolling Stones and ex-manager of Marianne Faithfull. I was called to the Mayfair office to meet him and sing some of my songs.

There I was surrounded by the theatrical plush typical of the day, the swags of red velvet and golden tassels, a grand piano with silver-framed signed photographs from grateful and loving clients, a white marble fireplace with an ornate electric bar fire, Mrs Mackey sitting silently behind her large desk – and there was Andrew, standing, shining, with his back to the mantelpiece and gilt-framed mirror. I doubt we exchanged glances and there were no words. Me – long white socks, small skirt, holey jumper, old guitar, moody demeanour and a croaking voice. Andrew, blond and perfectly otherworldly, looking down – or at the ceiling.

Sent away after a few songs, I had no thought that anything would come of the meeting, but next day I was again summoned, this time to Andrew's office in Ivor Court at the other end of Gloucester Place. He handed me an acetate recording of the Rolling Stones' 'Some Things Just Stick in Your Mind'. This was to be my first single. A Mick Jagger and Keith Richards song.

'But I want to record *my* songs.'

One of mine could go on the B-side, said Andrew, and my second single could be one of my own. I was not happy. I went home and complained at my father. He said – quite uncharacteristically – 'Compromise, dear girl.'

* * *

I did. I set out on a path I had not planned, but it surely had its moments.

The contrast between the traditional impresarios' world that I had glimpsed through our neighbours the Blacks and their friends, with this – Andrew Loog Oldham sweeping it all aside, wresting the reins and reclaiming music for the young – warmed my contrary little heart. I was just twenty, Andrew a year older. He had already brought the Stones to dazzling success and I was surely dazzled, but also aware that

I was around something quite world-changing, and I was quietly delighting in being a small part of the big fuck-you.

As much as I was terrified by them all – Andrew and his wordless way with me, Mick Jagger imitating my small voice with his head to the side and both hands together to his ear, the many, many musicians all crowded into the studio – it felt good that these young people were taking the place of the old.

Big Jim Sullivan, John McLaughlin and Jimmy Page on guitars and Nicky Hopkins on piano. I still have the handwritten scores from that day – the David Whitaker arrangements for 'Some Things Just Stick in Your Mind' and 'I Want To Be Alone' – all there, except for the piano since Nicky Hopkins improvised. So many instruments. I remember clearly the crowded studio, with the three trombones taking up the most space, the violins, violas and the harpsichord, the flugel horns, six-string bass guitar, finger cymbals, scraper, octamarimba – the list goes on.

Andrew Loog Oldham strode this new world with an irreverential grace. He made me laugh when I wasn't weeping. Later, it swelled my heart as I watched him walk up to a stiffly uniformed doorman in a Park Lane hotel, holding a large joint and asking for a light before sweeping out through the revolving door into the London streets – in a cloud of illicit smoke.

In a letter to my sister, I confessed to being 'a little in love with Andrew', but since he and I barely exchanged a word I remained a small skinny being, merging with the studio walls, silent, wide-eyed and almost not there.

I sang:

Why does the sky turn grey every night
Sun rise again in time
Why do you think of the first love you had
Some things just stick in your mind

Why does the rain fall down on the earth
Why do the clouds keep crying
Why do you sleep curled up like a child
Some things just stick in your mind

Why when the children grow up and leave
Still remember their nursery rhymes
Why must there be so much hate in their lives
Some things just stick in their minds

Mick Jagger and Keith Richards, 1965

* * *

As I slowly began to realise I was being promoted as Andrew's replacement for Marianne Faithfull I was angry and hurting. I thought of myself as a songwriter, a musician. I had my heart in the way that I sang and the songs that I was writing and I hated to be so dismissed as just a darker-haired, rather dumb version of Marianne. I was trying to make my own way, and I scowled at anyone who would listen that *she* didn't write her own songs.

Almost worse was being called a female Bob Dylan – as if I would ever have claimed or even thought that. What lessons I learned so young – that lies would be woven around me, facts embroidered at best, distorted at worst, and that journalists could write whatever they wanted to. The story grew and grew and I did not. The person I thought I was became someone else, someone quite unknown to me.

The single went nowhere. Andrew has since said that he thinks the B-side – my own song 'I Want to Be Alone' – was better. I thought so too, but I got into big trouble for saying on a radio show that I thought I wrote better songs than Mick Jagger. I meant for me to sing – but my penance was to have to paint the office walls and design a poster for The Poets. The idea was to keep me from getting above myself. Up a ladder. I was not allowed to tour either – in case it gave me ideas and ruined me, they said.

There were six weeks of appearances up and down the country for local TV stations. I failed the audition for

ITV's *Ready Steady Go!* but I was asked to be on their Saturday-night showing of *Thank Your Lucky Stars*. For that I was made to wear a black plastic raincoat and walk along the shore of the Thames, miming to the single that was being played on a Dansette record player in amongst the mud and stones. (No footage survives, apparently.)

Then there was the American TV show *Shindig*. They used to film some acts in the UK which they slotted in between the US acts, with canned audience applause and yelling. I had to mime again, and this time they said I had to move in time to the music. I don't move well, I wanted to just stand. I felt awkward and hated it. However, I was allowed to sit on a high stool for 'I Want to Be Alone'. Much better, probably because it was my song. No – I do not move well, never trusting the ground under my feet or the very air around me.

Many radio and press interviews and then – suddenly nothing. Pleading with the phone to ring. It didn't.

Two Roberts

Robert Hewison. We were sometimes together and sometimes not but that summer of 1965 we must have been, as we set off in his battered old green Austin A40 van, on our way to visit Mike Palin in Southwold.

Robert Lewis – a hitchhiker we picked up on that dark Suffolk night. He was walking with a large cardboard box under one arm and playing a harmonica with the other hand, when not sticking out a thumb.

'Get in the back, Vashti,' said Robert Hewison.

We had been planning to sleep in his van, but the other Robert invited us to stay the night at the old farm cottage he was renting whilst at art school in Ipswich. All I remember of the house are the Bob Dylan lyrics written over the walls along with some of Robert Lewis's own – and that there was no bathroom so I had to pee in a field for the first time in my life.

By morning he had gone. No note, just gone. It would be another year before he would return to our lives, to my life, forever.

Back in the studio Andrew had me record a song written by Jimmy Page. The promise that my second single would be one of my own songs seemed to have simply passed away. I sang the song badly, I didn't even try and it came to nothing.

So, there were months of more nothing over that winter, the family despairing of my promises that I would prove them wrong, moving between my parents' house and my brother's and back again. I spent time by hiring two reel-to-reel tape recorders so I could experiment with multi-tracking and building arrangements for the new songs I was writing.

'Winter Is Blue' came to me along with pneumonia, as Robert Hewison came and went. He was the inspiration for many of my songs over that time. I should have written one called 'Get in the Back, Vashti'.

At one time Andrew had put me in a room in the office with a record player, a piano and three albums – Tim Hardin, the Mamas & the Papas and the Beach Boys' *Pet Sounds*, with instruction to write something 'in between all of them'. I don't play the piano. I escaped, taking the records with me. I kept them.

And I wrote 'I'd Like to Walk Around in Your Mind'.

I'd like to walk around in your mind someday
I'd like to walk all over the things you say to me
I'd like to run and jump on your solitude
I'd like to rearrange your attitude to me

You say you just want peace and to never hurt anyone
You see the end before the beginning has ever begun

I would disturb your easy tranquillity
I'd turn away the sad impossibility of your smile

I'd sit there in the sun of the things I like about you
I'd sing my songs and find out just what they mean to you

But most of all I'd like you to be unaware
Then I'd just wander away
Trailing palm leaves behind me
So you don't even know that I've been there

Unreleased single for Immediate, 1966

Generations

I had met Alasdair Clayre in 1963, on a train going back to Oxford in my first year at the Ruskin. He was ten years older than me, at twenty-eight the youngest to be made a fellow of All Souls. He was an overwhelmingly intense person, unsettling to be with – I felt as if he was far too closely studying me. What with his tweed jacket and shiny brown brogues, I did not understand him at all. He wrote poems for me which he left in an empty milk bottle on my doorstep when I did not answer the bell. I wonder if he knew I was hiding from him as I heard his Vespa scooter stopping at my door.

However, through that winter of 1965 and '66, the winter of the silent phone, I did regret my unkindness, get to know him better and appreciate his words at least. The tune to Jenny Lewis's and my song '17 Pink Sugar Elephants' just happened to fit one of Alasdair's poems which became 'Train Song'. Two other songs, 'Girl's Song in Winter' and 'If in Winter' were from poems written by Alasdair, with amended words and tunes added by me.

He by now lived in a long, dark loft in the East End of London where I sat wordlessly amongst people who were loudly talking about the meanings of their poetry. It was that kind of talk where everyone spoke but no one listened and it couldn't hold my slight interest for long. They were all a lot older than me, and had neither understanding nor time for the world of popular music. Alasdair introduced me to

Cecil Sharp House and that very particular folk music that is steeped in tradition – pickled in aspic as I saw it. The tunes I liked, but the instrumentation and the whole feel of the folk world did not sit well with me. I could find no place in it – nor was any kind of place made for me.

We were a whole generation apart at a time when it *mattered*.

My generation, so different. Post-war children, with no need to know of the terrors and hardships the older ones had witnessed. We were fortunate, safe, protected for sure, but heartened in a way that enabled us to ignore the constraints and seemingly insufferable and incomprehensible moralities which still bound those who had gone before us.

Being told constantly that I should be toeing the line made no sense to me, especially since there was no real explanation of what that line might look like, as if no one really knew any more – and so crossing it just became a way of life.

Signed

I rented a small bedsit in the top of a house in Queen Anne Street, around the corner from my brother in Harley Street.

It had a beautiful curved window and view over the chimney pots and untidy London roofs, old red brick, rusty iron fire escape ladders, and faraway imagined hills.

A knock on my bedsit door, and my landlady showed in a bald middle-aged man who came and sat on my bed. I was still asleep in it. He was from the government, he said, and he told me I had not made the required number of National Insurance contributions since leaving education. I imagine that all he could see of me was my eyes above the eiderdown, and I had nothing to say – not having much understanding of how these things worked. He told me that if I didn't pay up what I owed, and start to pay a weekly contribution, I would have to forego ever having any kind of pension, or maternity benefit or anything at all from the government, and I must sign this piece of paper he was handing me – to say I understood I would get nothing, ever. Thinking I would do anything to get this man off my bed I stretched out an arm from under the bedclothes – and signed it.

I never did pay in, and I didn't claim maternity benefit and I don't claim a pension now.

At least he went.

Ephemeral

By this time my brother was my greatest advocate. He recorded some of my recent songs on his new reel-to-reel machine, always frustrated that no one else seemed to know what I was on about. He had a friend who was Ewan MacColl and Peggy Seeger's agent and arranged for me to meet them to ask for advice as to what I should do next. So, I took my guitar and my songs, went to their house and sat on the edge of a sofa. They were both very solemn. I sang, and they remained very solemn. Unsmiling, they didn't say anything. But it became obvious in the silence that I was going to have to go, and as I got up Peggy Seeger opened the door for me and said, 'All I can say is, beware of the ephemeral.'

I didn't have any idea what she meant. What's an 'ephemeral'? Was I to fear it may jump out at me from around the corner? I looked it up when I got home. Oh. That's exactly what I *mean*. That's exactly what I like about pop songs, that they capture a moment and then you move on to the next one. The way that at just twenty-one years old I had learned that love moves on, and so do record producers.

Gone tomorrow, here today

'Don't Believe What They Say',
Some Things Just Stick in Your Mind, 1963

But then I met a Canadian producer called Peter Snell. He was taken with the recent songs and bought me out of my contract with Andrew. Peter is one person from that time that I haven't been able to find – I would like so much to be able to thank him. He understood my original quieter ideals, so 'Train Song' and 'Love Song' were recorded with a session guitarist, cellist and double bassist only, in contrast to the enormous backing of Andrew's productions. It came out as a single on Columbia in May 1966, and was played once on pirate Radio Caroline (where copies were given away as a competition prize), but without much in the way of promotion it had no chance.

One person who did hear it was Robert Lewis, the hitchhiker from Suffolk. He wrote me a letter on brown paper and addressed it to 'Vashti, Decca Records, London'.

'Train Song' was on Columbia, not Decca as my first single had been, but a while later I was in Andrew's office and a secretary there handed me an envelope that had been in a drawer in her desk. Someone at Decca had sent it over. Robert Lewis was now living in London, and studying at Ravensbourne College of Art. Robert Hewison and I went to find him and later in this story it will be clear that he (Robert Lewis) figured largely in my life – and that my three children are thanks to a secretary in Andrew's office who cared enough to pass on a letter.

———

Blue

Meanwhile – back in my world of aching for my songs to be heard – Alasdair Clayre had invited me to sing at a poetry reading in the ICA (Institute of Contemporary Arts) on Dover Street, London.

I was terrified, but John Martyn was on ahead of me, and so watching his complete irreverence towards the audience was a revelation. The vision of the glass of beer by his side, the lit cigarette he slowly and deliberately stuck on the end of a stray string-end sticking out from the head of his guitar and the smoke lazily curling around him in the spotlight, stayed with me. I picked up the habit of having a lit cigarette stuck on a stray string-end when writing songs, every new line needing a quick draw to stay the panic and steel the nerve.

After the ICA poetry reading Alasdair told me that a friend of his, an American record producer named Joe Boyd, had been in the audience and wanted to talk to me about making an album. Joe tried to call me, but I didn't go to meet him. If I had done, things might have been very different, but I had so missed the world I'd glimpsed through Andrew Loog Oldham that all it took was a phone call from his partner Tony Calder and I was back in the office of their new independent label Immediate. The duo Twice as Much had a hit with the Jagger/Richards song 'Sittin' on A Fence', and Tony said, 'There you are, you see – if you hadn't gone off to try it by yourself, you could have had that one.' Again I scowled. 'But I want to record *my* songs.'

Tony, quietly, 'How does she expect me to sell poetry?'

Poetry?

Some of my songs had simple arrangements that I had worked out with a guitarist called Mike Crowther. Andrew chose 'Winter Is Blue' and asked Art Greenslade to arrange it for an enormous orchestra, with an operatic diva singing a long note in the middle. Art changed a bit of the vocal melody too, which would have had me very much objecting a year before, but I was beginning to lose the huge confidence in my songs that I had started out with, and just let them do it.

I was still somewhat in awe of them all but just once I found the courage to say I thought the guitar parts that Mike and I had written for the beginning of 'Winter Is Blue' needed to be played a bit softer. They weren't – and I don't think I said another word.

Peter Whitehead was at the first session, filming for his *Tonite Let's All Make Love in London* documentary, which all went over my head. The Small Faces were there that night, with P. P. Arnold recording, and I remember hanging on her every note.

I thought the recording of 'Winter Is Blue' went well, but the next day Andrew wasn't happy and we had another try. To me, the second attempt didn't sound as good, but it's the one that ended up on the *Tonite Let's All Make Love in London* soundtrack. It seemed to me at those sessions that everybody would work hard and long into the night, and at the end, when everything was done and we were listening back, it sounded so good up in this little smoky booth in the middle of the night. And then I think maybe when they listened back to 'Winter Is Blue' in the cold light of day it just didn't sound anything like it had in that euphoric atmosphere of the studio. And so, we went back to do it again, to try and recapture something, and maybe losing what we had in the first place.

At the end of one long night, when everyone was happily sitting back and listening, the doors opened down in the dark, empty studio and in came two policemen with flashing torches. The crackle of real fear that went around that little booth was highly relieved when they shouted up to us that somebody had left their car lights on.

'Winter Is Blue' was meant to be a single, but one day I was called to the office and Tony Calder told me they weren't going to release it because Cliff Richard wanted the song. I never believed him, but when I recently told Andrew he said, 'Well, you know, it just might have been true.' As he pointed out, Cliff Richard did cover a Stones song ('Blue Turns to Grey'), so it seems that Tony could have tragically (for me) got the two confused and thought my 'Winter Is Blue' was actually theirs.

Everything was moving so fast for everyone involved with Immediate, and I think that a lot just got lost in the tide. Like me. And now that I know what probably happened, well, I can't be angry with someone who is gone. RIP Tony.

If my heart freezes,
I won't feel the breaking.

'Winter Is Blue',
Some Things Just Stick in Your Mind, 1966

I got a dog. I called him Blue – after the winter.

Coldest Night

Soon I was summoned again, to meet Andrew's duo Twice
as Much and start rehearsing 'Coldest Night of the Year',
which was going to be released under the name Twice As

Much & Vashti. We didn't write it – it's a Mann–Weil Brill Building composition that another Immediate band, the Factotums, had recorded and never released.

These were my best days at Immediate, rehearsing and being able to input ideas. We wanted a Beach Boys kind of sound, and I think we got it. We had worked it out in Andrew's Park Lane hotel room. Brian Jones was causing concern at the time, and everyone seemed worried about what was to happen with him. He came in at one point, looking so ill, and desperate, really. Voices lowered to whispers. As always, I sat, quiet, with wide eyes, and witnessed this extraordinary play being acted out, different Stones drifting in and out of the room whilst Andrew Rose, David Skinner and I rehearsed the song over and over till Andrew Oldham was satisfied.

The recording was made at Pye, and I love it still. Gered Mankowitz photographed the three of us up on Primrose Hill, but the single never happened and I was not told why. I didn't hear of it again until years later when I was away up the country behind a black horse and I somehow found out that the track was included on the second Twice as Much album, released in 1968. I expect by that time I was not giving much of a shit about the Immediate days gone by.

The Last Time

1967. I was on my way to giving up on Immediate and letting another girl singer have all my songs when Tony Calder got wind of it and asked to hear them.

Mike Hurst was producing for Immediate and so Tony Calder gave him me, and my songs. We recorded 'I'd Like to Walk Around in Your Mind' and I was as sure as could be that this was it, this was all I'd ever wanted to sound like, thank you Mike. When Andrew heard it, he said it needed strings and much more filling out. We tried, it didn't work, it got swept aside as before and I was left with just an acetate demo of that first recording.

In the years and months and days between all these recording sessions which came to nothing there were loves and lovers who disappeared like snow in spring, leaving me reeling but still willing to try it all over again.

Until this time though, with the latest Immediate shelving, the most recent heartbreak, and the little ghosts of lost babies whose stories will never be told, I now felt I had nowhere to go.

There was no advantage taken that was not freely given, there is no blame, but by now I was a concern to my family with my downward-spiralling despair. Between my brother and my New York psychoanalyst brother-in-law it was thought a good idea to send me to a place they called the

Castle – described to me as 'a nut-house for creative people'. I said no. Who would look after my dog?

Instead, I went to stay with my father's sister who was married to the GP doctor in Leek, Staffordshire. I had spent many summers with them as a child and I knew them well. They looked after me, cared for me, asked me no questions and I had no lies to tell. My uncle was a quiet, gentle man who took me on his rounds visiting his patients every afternoon. These rounds often involved going to look at sites he had identified as having been visited by the ancient Egyptians. He was obsessed with ley lines (the first I had heard of them) and pored over *The Old Straight Track* and maps with me, quite sure I believed every word the same as he did. Why would I doubt him? There was no room for it.

As he was seeing a patient one of the days, I stayed in the car, parked on a ridge looking out over the wildness of the Roaches.

The Roaches (or Roches) is a wind-carved outcrop of gritstone rocks.

The sky was wide, filled with layers of grey clouds, some dark and some silver-bright, moving towards me fast on the wind, beautiful. But suddenly – very suddenly – I couldn't reach the feeling of beauty. I was removed from it, separated, alone, petrified on the edge of an abyss that I had never known was there. From that moment on I would know it was there and would either feel I was treading a high wire above it, or else falling – with nowhere to land.

Learn to Fall

Before my return to London my aunt came down from the attic with a torn and dusty black case containing a small bird's eye maple guitar with mother-of-pearl flowers inlaid around the sound hole.

'I thought you might like to have this old banjo thing,' she said.

I took the old thing away with me, but fervently vowed not to sing, write songs or record in a studio, no, not ever again.

That little guitar would go on to change all that, but for now I applied to the Slade School of Art. I was rejected. I answered an advertisement for an animal nurse posted by a vet just off Kings Road. A pound a day and 14/6d on Saturday mornings. He wanted a school-leaver – he said I was overqualified – but I pleaded that I really wanted this job. He took me on, so I set about cleaning and rearranging his long-time dusty shelves full of brown bottles with faded labels, some stuck to the old paint – not having been moved for years. He was astonished, but it was good for me to be tidying and sorting, and trying to do the same to my mind. There was also some peace in the focus on small creatures needing their own fears calmed.

Invited to a party with recently made friends – over the road from my parents – I was given a strange-tasting drink as I arrived. Next thing I knew I was being pulled back from climbing out of the window, three floors up. I was deposited back home, never to see any of them again, nor to know what it was in that glass.

Family doctor said I was hypoglycaemic and that my foot was stuck on the accelerator pedal, so he put me on a diet of bananas and steak. I lasted a week but was not noticeably any better and so he put me on Librium, Valium and a new antidepressant. Did it calm me down? No. Wherever I went I had to leave immediately. I could not keep still. The only relief was climbing up the down escalator at Marble Arch tube station. At least I stayed in the same place.

Screaming at my mother that no one could see this kind of agony, no one could know it and the worst was that I could not describe it – she went downstairs to the office to see if there was any milk in the fridge there so she could make me some cocoa. She had a stroke on the way back up.

I stopped taking the pills.

* * *

My mother did not know me any more. After the stroke she had then been diagnosed with a rare condition needing instant open-heart surgery. Found also to have cancer she had a hysterectomy, after which she had terrible undiagnosable pain. They gave her electric shock treatment.

I stayed home, looking after a heartbroken and half-crazed father who one minute was a big man crying and the next was standing over his wife's hospital bed imploring her to remember where she had put the key to the safe. She had been saving up for some new curtains.

Robert Lewis (the Suffolk hitch-hiker, now at Ravensbourne College of Art) had invited me to the opening of a show of his friend Anthony Benjamin's sculptures. At the after-show dinner we all sat at a long table and I asked Robert what the point of all this was and the whole table fell silent. We became friends.

Night after night he stood at the hospital door with Blue on a lead, sometimes in the rain, waiting for me as I visited my mother. He then sat with me at the kitchen table. I had never known such kindness but he had no way of knowing the terrible dread I had of not only the very unsound ground beneath my feet, but also by now of the sky and the stars and the infinite dark of the universe.

One night Robert muttered some words at me in a language I didn't understand. He then told me he had put a spell on me, that I would never leave his side. My terrified brain – post-prescription drugs and dealing with the sudden disappearance of a recognisable mother – went into freefall.

* * *

Fall into sleep, as the sun comes up,
and wake at the back of noon,
Drift through the hours as the sun gets lower
'til the days are lit by the moon.

'Across the Water', *Heartleap*, 2010

Next day, after a wakeful night dropping and dropping through space, I was awoken at the back of noon by a furious father yelling that my dog had crapped in the doorway of his surgery when a patient was due, and that the dog had to go. Or I had to go.

I had to go.

Into the Wood

I needed a way to keep my dog and not lose my mind. Or my life. What would Blue do without me? I left home, with the pound note that my father had given me after I had told him that my best idea was to go to live in a bush in a wood somewhere – with an art student I barely knew.

In that early summer of 1968 I took the bus to Bromley Common and followed the directions that Robert Lewis had given me, past Ravensbourne College of Art, down a long path into a wood. I stood with my dog on a lead in one hand and a pillow and plaid blanket under my other arm, looking up into a small birch tree where Robert was stretching a canvas between its branches with garden twine. He had already tied a canvas under a large rhododendron bush, which I was about to move into with him. He looked uncertain.

He was in his last semester at the art school which he attended against his parents' will, he had little money and so nowhere to live and was tired of asking to sleep on other people's floors.

He had a diploma show to set up at the college, which was to be the table and chairs he made in the wood and his beautiful leafy paintings on the stretched canvasses in the trees. He says he was 'living underneath a picture and then making life the picture'.

* * *

Robert had laid a small square of carpet on the earth in the bush, and on top of that there was a single green mattress. I added my pillow and blanket. We gathered a saucepan, breadboard and knives over the days from local junk shops, I found a roll of white muslin and made curtains to go around the whole house. We cooked young nettles in the old saucepan over the fire. We needed salt, which we took from the art-school canteen.

I had been home to collect some clothes, things, and my little guitar. I wrote a song.

> Glow worms show the path we have to tread
> Dreamers, we should be asleep in bed
> Moving slowly through the springtime air
> Holding moments in the depth of care
> Holding moments in the depth of care
>
> Whisper fairy stories till they're real
> Wonder how the night can make us feel
> Loving living more with love to stay
> Long past sadness that was in our way
> Long past sadness that was in our way
>
> Dawntime mist begins reflecting light
> Waking sun will soon forget our night
> Love me through the day and I'll with you go
> Into summer and the next year's snow
> Into summer and the next year's snow

'Glow Worms', *Just Another Diamond Day*, 1968

Rose

Robert's art-school friend John James came to sit by our fire sometimes, drinking maté tea with us, saying little as Robert said much. When John did speak it was to clearly and succinctly sweep away all the general assumptions Robert tended to make, leaving me wide-eyed with admiration.

Happily for me John had a nearby mother. A visit to Rose's house meant pie and beans for us within minutes of arrival, and after a few penniless days in the wood eating nettle soup with someone who was not at all sure I should be there, and whom I was not at all sure I should be with, I looked forward to seeing Rose. She was a great comfort as she reminded me of the best things about my own mother. Dark-haired and dark-eyed, direct, generous and funny.

Rose had three sons; John was the youngest. They lived in a long road of semi-detached houses in Barnehurst, identical but for Rose's. There were the remains of two 1930s Austin 12s in the front garden, some of whose parts had gone to make up the third – Happiness Runs (named after a Donovan song) – which stood at the door. John's enormous paintings were stacked up the stairs and throughout the house so that one room looked much like another. The upright piano was painted with one coat of pale-blue emulsion. Desmond Dekker and the Aces played loudly as John's father sat wordlessly at the table in the window and his mother cooked and chatted and bustled.

With no words or judgement Rose would bring a morning tray of tea and lay it beside Robert's head and mine as we slept on the floor in John's bedroom, John fully clothed in his bed with his boots on and wearing a top hat. It was a room crammed with everything that Rose had ever bought at a jumble sale, like two large cardboard boxes of size ten ladies' shoes; more of John's paintings, some of Robert's; Robert's clocks. He bought and sold them, along with silver pocket watches, ethnic weapons and oil lamps, to pay his way through art school.

Two Blue Men

On our return one dark night to our rhododendron home we found that our bed had been soaked in paraffin from the oil lamp, and Robert's best silver pocket watch was gone. There was no way to get back to John's house so late, so we stung all night and in the morning awoke to boy voices. Robert was in his ankle-length Victorian nightshirt, he had very long hair and he shot from the bush in his bare feet waving a Fijian war club and roaring as loud as his rage would let him. The boys went white and fled, stumbling through the trees with Robert crashing behind them. He came back looking pleased with himself.

* * *

Half an hour later we had a visit from two policemen and a man in a grey suit. The representative of the Bank of England – whose land we were on – politely asked us to leave. 'What if everyone were to want to come and live here?'

What indeed.

The two policemen meanwhile had been rummaging in our rhododendron-bush home, and emerged triumphant with a crumpled and long-ignored court summons which Robert had amongst his few belongings. He had been stopped three times between London and Suffolk on an uninsured, untaxed motorbike with just a learner plate which would not have allowed him to have a pillion passenger. He did.

We were ordered to pack everything up and were then escorted to the far edge of the wood. Our small green world with birds and primroses there opened out into a housing estate where the new white houses gleamed, straight-sided and raw. This was where the boys had come from, had run ashen-faced and screaming back to, and from where their parents had phoned the police, reporting a wild man in the woods. Robert was handcuffed to one of the officers who was talking on his radio, whilst the other asked me if I had anywhere to go whilst Robert got a few months inside.

The summons was more than six months old, a small detail they had overlooked, and so, apparently, we were free. The police car sulkily drove away, leaving us standing on the side of the road with the dog, my guitar, an oil lamp, saucepan and a bow saw, a Fijian war club, bright green mattress, blanket, pillow and a Georgian silver teapot lid.

The rest of that teapot had been hurled by a raging Robert into a bush when he'd seen that I had accidentally melted a hole in the spout when warming it by the fire. He had ripped off the lid first, and years later, when I knew about these things, I saw that the hallmark could have told us that he had owned a very valuable London-made piece of silver which would probably have paid all of Robert's long-owed art-school fees and left us some over to rent a house with. How different things might have been.

As it was, I walked to the phone box to sadly summon John and Happiness Runs. Whilst we piled all our household goods into the back it came to us that a good way to get over our present problems would be to have a house permanently on wheels. 'What about petrol?' asked John, who had a problem with it in that he only put a little at a time into his car on the basis that the less he put in the less she would use.

'We'd need a horse,' said Robert.

Happiness ran out of petrol.

We all knew the shortest route to the nearest garage by now so got out to push. As we were resting at the side of the Sidcup bypass, leaning against the back of the car in the evening sun, I caught a glimpse of an old wheel through a gap in the fence. On closer inspection we found that it belonged to a broken-down horse-drawn baker's van with a canopy over the front seat and little oval windows in the side. Ten yards away was a new bright-white and chrome Traveller's van with cut-glass sprays of flowers on the windows and a half-door. Over this door leant a large man who watched us coldly.

'We're looking for a cart like this, is it for sale?'

'Might be.'

'Do you know where we could find a horse for it?'

'Come back in the morning.'

Pegasus

That night, with Rose's pies and beans, we planned a journey. We would go west or north, maybe as far as Cornwall, or even Scotland, until we could find a place that no one could tell us to leave. We would earn a living along the way doing anything we could. Painting houses, digging gardens, cleaning windows. People might join us; we could put on shows on village greens. We could paint, we could write. The dogs would be free (John had a rough collie called Swanney), and we could have chickens, maybe even a cow. It was a long night and I dreamt of Pegasus with white wings and long mane flying, carrying me away from all my dark and fearful feelings, away to another land, another life.

The morning brought apprehension. Mr Ball was big and said nothing but led us to a small rounded shed, an Anderson bomb shelter left over from the war. He pulled back the door and all that we could see in the gloom was a large black backside and a short, docked tail. As this horse turned her head over her shoulder to look at us we could see a white star on her forehead. She was lying in straw but a sound from Mr Ball brought her backing out of the shed, shuffling on her knees, then standing and shaking herself out. She was stout, strong-looking and had hairy feet. She was disdainful and proud. I was in complete awe of her; she knew it all, and I knew almost nothing about horses.

She was put into harness and attached to a small flat cart

with a high seat at the front. Robert was invited up with just a jerk of a chin, his face and knuckles going white as Alfie Ball clicked his tongue and the horse leapt away up the lane with Robert's hair streaking behind them.

They came back a few minutes later more sedately and we found the courage to ask how much.

'A hundred and fifty pounds, horse, van and harness.' Mr Ball ambled back to his caravan, smoking his pipe. He knew he had us. 'Don't keep looking as if you want her,' hissed Robert, who clearly knew more about dealing than I did. I didn't want to appear rude and said I thought she was beautiful. Robert sighed and said we'd think about it.

I was in pain trying to think of any way we could find that kind of money when we had really nothing.

———

However to Find One Hundred and Fifty Pounds

My mother's sister Dorothy had died recently. I knew that she had left each of her nieces and nephews £100 each and that her brother, my Uncle William, was the executor of her estate. I hoped he might tell me I could have my legacy now, so John took us in Happiness Runs down to the house in Rochester, Kent, where a surprised Aunt Kathleen opened the door to a niece she had not seen in years, dressed in a long green cloak with black button boots, and accompanied by what must have looked like two characters out of a western and a Viking saga.

John's cowboy boots had worn down at the heel so much that the toes curled upwards and he wore a suit that he had run up on his mother's sewing machine out of an old brown tweed blanket. He had paint in his shaggy black hair, said not a word and looked out of his beautiful face with dark eyes. Robert had long straight blond hair and wore a large black cloak. His calf-length leather boots had also seen better days and the soles flapped.

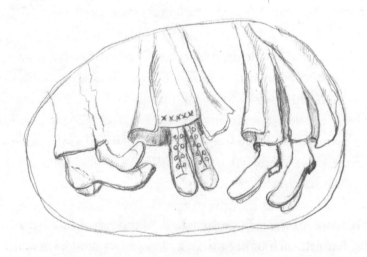

This aunt whom I had always found a little stern and whom I half expected to turn us away, welcomed us in and fed us. The bad news from my uncle that the money from Aunt Dorothy's will could not come through for another two months was softened by my being shown into the garage where all her worldly goods were laid out ready to go to the jumble sale. I was told to take whatever I wanted and so I collected up old lace, silk nightdresses, velvet jackets and frocks from the 1920s, sheets, blankets, pillows, a teapot, everything we could possibly need to make our lives with.

We piled up the car with all that we could, and went back to John's house, wondering where to spend the next two weeks until Robert's diploma show, where to put all our new possessions and how to come up with £150.

*   *   *

Two painting students, friends of Robert's, had a flat near to the art school and they kindly offered to let us stay. There was an old door lying in their hall cupboard, which we balanced horizontally on the middle one of the shelves that ran round the three sides. On the top and bottom shelves we put everything we owned, and on the door we laid our green mattress.

We had Aunt Dorothy's sheets and blankets. We had candles. We had a home.

Whilst living in the cupboard and still wondering how to find £150 for horse, cart and harness, John James, Robert and I went to visit a family that Robert adored, at Gothic Farm in Suffolk.

Hugh and Cynthia had been conscientious objectors in

the war. Along with many others, they were given conditional exemption to work on the land or in forestry. It was possible then to buy empty farms cheaply so communities were formed with ideals of self-sufficiency and peace, away from the warfare state. Gothic Farm had been such a community, but Hugh and Cynthia bought out their other co-operators after the war was over. They continued to work the farm and bore four daughters. The second one, TO, had been Robert's girlfriend. He loved these people like they were his own family, which I'm sure he wished they were, since his own didn't seem to understand him one bit.

I'd always wanted to live in the country, but I had grown up in London and so being introduced to Robert's adoptive family had been difficult. I felt clumsy, frivolous and ignorant of their lives. The youngest daughter was having a birthday party and I stood by the huge open log fire biting into a small cake. It was very good, but it seemed a funny colour. 'What kind of flour is this made with?' I asked the child. 'Brown flour of course.' She looked at me as if I were quite stupid and walked away.

I had never known of brown anything except Hovis bread. I soon learned, as brown rice, flour, sugar and even brown paper were to become the staples of our lives.

Gothic Farm looked as if it had been sea-bleached throughout, like driftwood. All the walls were white, with the unpainted kitchen furniture taken out every Saturday and scrubbed. The worn red-brick floor in the kitchen had a drain in the middle and was also scrubbed by the whole family on Saturdays whilst the furniture was outside. Everything in the house was beautiful in a faded way – soft, worn and looked after.

The fireplace was so big that Hugh would carry in a tree limb over his shoulder and place it across the embers till it caught. As it burned in the middle the two ends would be pushed towards each other, until it was time to get another piece of tree from outside.

Cynthia was a potter. Everything that was used at the table had been made by her. The very house looked as if it had come from the earth, or the sea, but quietly and in no way shown off, in no way prescriptive of anyone else's way. Well, no, that's not quite true. I always felt unworthy.

I loved Cynthia but was quite in awe of her. My main memory of her is from a short visit a year (and what felt like a lifetime) later, when she was sitting on the old swing in the garden and I went to talk to her. I told her my mother had just died.

'Mothers do.'

How High

On the Sunday of my first visit to Gothic Farm a loud vehicle drew up outside, the stable door to the kitchen flew open and in strode a procession of the wildest looking band of people dressed in Afghan coats and velvet jackets, bells and beads and patchwork, blinding colours against the mellow interior of the farmhouse.

It was Donovan Leitch and his friends. Old friends, schoolfriends, one of whom had been at Ravensbourne College with Robert and John – Sam, Donovan's 'Skip-A-Long Sam', a beautiful, delicate painter.

They were all bursting with tales of the islands that Donovan had just bought off the Isle of Skye in western Scotland, a small part of the main part of Skye too, with some derelict cottages and an old schoolhouse.

Donovan sang, 'How high the gulls fly o'er Islay'.

I was swept up, as was Robert, into this great gale of ideas for a future of like-minded people going to live in a remote and northerly part of the United Kingdom – far away from the problems of trying to find a way to live in London. Not a community so much as a collection of sympathetic people – painters, musicians, writers, all free to make their artistry their lives – they said. A West Coast Renaissance, Donovan said.

We should go with them. But how? Donovan and his friends had a Land Rover to go up in. Robert and I had nothing. We told them about our finding a small wagon and a black horse called Betsy, and so the idea of the two of us and Blue, or three of us with John and his dog Swanney, going up there on foot seemed to appeal to everyone, none of us in these our wildest dumb dreams figuring that walking might take us a lot longer to get there.

I arranged to borrow a hundred pounds from Donovan with a promise to pay him back once my inheritance had come through.

* * *

Robert sold his grandfather clock to Robert Hewison for thirty-five pounds. Back we went to see Alfred Ball and his horse.

Robert Lewis – the dealer. I was again instructed to stay quiet as we approached Mr Ball in the field where the horse he called Betsy was standing on the end of a long chain attached to a leather collar around her neck. I again said I thought she was beautiful and Robert narrowed his eyes at me.

I remember clearly an offer being made that was way less than the hundred and fifty asked, and Mr Ball looking disgusted, throwing the chain on the ground and walking away. I was devastated and thought it the end of everything but Robert glared at me to say nothing, upped his offer a little and sealed the deal for one hundred and thirty-five pounds.

Robert – by now not inclined to put his name to anything official – had me write out the receipt, slowly dictated by Mr Ball, then signed by him over six one-penny postage stamps.

I the undersigned have sold the horse Betsy, the cart and harness to Miss Vashti Bunyan on July 3rd 1968, and she accepts all responsibility for these items from this date forward.

In receipt of £135 . 0s . 0d

Alfred ...

* * *

Harnessing a horse is quite easy once it is learned – and learn it we had to, fast.

Moving out of the cupboard via Happiness Runs into the wagon, old and brown, leaning to one side and with one broken shaft – felt like just another anchor lost, just another leap off a cliff, but by now I was beginning to get used to them. The ground a little more trustworthy, the sky no longer as daunting, the stars not quite diamonds in the sky – but getting there.

My first lesson in the way Travelling People were treated – and still are – came as we crossed London Bridge heading north, possibly the last horse-drawn vehicle to cross the bridge before it was bought by an American industrialist and taken away to Arizona stone by stone. A car full of young men overtook us, hooting their horn and yelling out of the windows. I couldn't hear their words. I didn't need to. The ugliness of their contorted faces was enough to convey the hatred they felt for us.

Betsy walked on. She must have heard it all before.

———

Shoes

Our first stop in London was in Islington where Robert's one-time tutor and now friend Anthony Benjamin had a large home and studio. We parked the wagon on the side of the street, walked Betsy through to the back garden and let her loose on the grass.

Anthony and Nancy's upstairs neighbour was a sculptor whose artwork stood about the garden. Big welded sheets of sharp rusting iron were perfect for Betsy to scratch her backside against, making them rock. The second-floor window shot up and the sculptor shouted at us to 'get that fucking horse off my work'. I thought it was funny but his shaking fist and red face made me have to learn to be a bit sorry and so we tied her up in another part of the garden.

Deciding that this was the beginning of the next part of our lives we emptied our possessions from the wagon onto the grass and went through it all, making a bonfire of everything that was not important any longer. Like all my writing and all Robert's writing. Pretty shoes no good for walking in. Books that would be heavy for the horse.

I often think of that bonfire and all that we lost of our young selves. Robert leant in and rescued a few pieces of paper. I have them still, burned around the edges.

Betsy lost a shoe.

Islington High Street, London, July 1968

I wore my late aunt's 1930s nightdress, nothing else. Nothing on my feet and a pink crêpe bias-cut flower-printed night-dress long enough to trip me if I didn't hold it up. My hair was long too – dark brown, unbrushed – and I led a fat black horse with a white star on her forehead, a short tail and one missing shoe.

My main concern was that she should not tread on my toes, but her big feet were always thoughtfully placed. Later on I would watch her as she ate from a bucket of oats in a farmyard with small yellow chicks pecking up the grains that spilled from her mouth. She trod carefully between them all.

My feet had always been safe.

Right now we needed a blacksmith and our directions took us down Islington High Street, with people staring out of buses and stopping on the pavements to watch us go by as we looked for the Whitbread Brewery. There, we were told, they had a stable of grey shire horses who – six at a time – pulled the giant drays around the streets delivering barrels of ale to the pubs. These horses had their own forge up in the far corner of their stable, a stable as large in scale as they were with their names like High, Gog and Magog and their feet the size of frying pans.

'Hello Bess,' said the blacksmith as we walked towards the forge – the dusty sun in my eyes from the big high windows.

We thought her name was Betsy. The Romany Alfie Ball who had sold her to us the day before had called her Betsy.

'Na – that's old Bess – I'd know her anywhere.'

Old?

We'd had a friend who knew about horses give her a looking over and she'd been pronounced young enough, about ten maybe, but it turned out that Bess must have been born before the law against docking horses' tails was passed, making her twenty or more. The blacksmith showed us how her teeth proved his point. She had seemingly lived her long life out on the streets of London pulling delivery vans. Bakers, grocers and latterly a flower seller had all taught her traffic wisdom, which was just as well for us when she stopped at traffic lights, and went the right way around roundabouts.

The smith made four shoes of iron red-hot from the fire, banging them into shape on the anvil whilst telling us she would need them specially built up on account of her habit of turning her back feet with every step. This would wear her shoes down quickly, he said.

He didn't ask us for any money, just a tune or a song. Robert looked at me – the singer – but I turned my head away. Robert had a harmonica in his pocket and so played a bit of a tune and danced around the stable in his boots with the flapping soles. I watched through my fingers, in my pink nightdress, thinking how can a grown man dance like that, as if around a toadstool, without feeling daft. He didn't mind at all. I think at that moment he thought himself a little person, small and elven with leggings and perfect pointed soft green shoes.

Everyone there, the blacksmith, the stable boys and the dray drivers all enjoyed the show, we made our grateful goodbyes and I led Betsy – the little old horse we had thought so large that morning – out past the soaring grey backsides of the Whitbread shires and into the Islington streets.

She would be Bess from now on – her real, old name.

Seagull's Rest

We had a map showing us the way north. Our first stop outside London was on Barnet Common, the best bit of grass we could find. With nowhere to tie Bess, we tied her to the wagon.

There was a backboard on the wagon which when let down and hitched up with a chain horizontal to the wagon floor made a space just big enough for our green mattress to be mostly inside but partly sticking out of the back. There was a red and white striped awning hanging down from the back of the roof, just long enough to cover our feet at the end of our bed and shelter us from the wind and rain.

In the morning Bess's big black head came through the awning, took hold of our blankets with her teeth and pulled them off. We were exposed to the stares of early dog walkers.

Before anyone had the chance to report us and have us moved on, we were gone, back out onto the road and heading for Donovan's house – Seagull's Rest in Hertfordshire.

We planned to make the wagon more roadworthy there. The roof leaked, one spring was snapped, one shaft was broken, and the whole wagon was painted brown – that wartime colour that is all the leftover paints mixed up together – a kind of non-colour.

One of Donovan's friends perfectly mended the roof with proper roofing felt. Only later did we realise how much heavier it made the wagon – but by then it was too late.

A disused rolling pin was found to mend the broken end of the shaft. I hold this grudge – maybe unfairly – but for me it is emblematic of the future battles I would have with Robert. He had very cleverly spliced the rolling pin onto the end of the broken shaft and then it was my job to shape it to match the other one. I was halfway there when Robert said I should stop.

'But it still looks like a rolling pin,' I said, carrying on, needing to make it as much like the other as I could, wanting it perfect. No, I had to stop, as he said I would make it too thin and it would not be strong enough.

'But it needs to match – it looks all wrong.'

I gave in. It was painted with the rest, and still looked like – a rolling pin. Every time we harnessed the horse I scowled about it with the dark thought that Robert could not have me make something the way I wanted, the way I knew I could.

Soon the spring was mended, the body of the wagon

VASHTI BUNYAN

was painted green, the undercarriage and shafts red and the
wheels yellow. Sam Richards and John James – Robert's art
school friends – painted on the walls inside, small dreamlike
landscapes of the places we were headed for.

Donovan was away most of the days recording *The
Hurdy Gurdy Man* (Sam painted the cover) and came and
went driving his huge horsebox. He always arrived back with
presents for everybody there. For me, a pewter candlestick,
and one time a long purple velvet coat with many covered
buttons. With its wide shoulders, I think it must have been
made as part of a theatrical costume for a man, but I wore
it anyway.

He gave us each a copy of a book called *Miracles: Poems
by Children of the English-speaking World*, collected by
Richard Lewis. I still have mine, a survivor of many damp
barns and attics.

One poem has stayed with me always:

> *I love animals and dogs and everything*
> *But how can I do it when dogs are dead and*
>   *a hundred?*
> *But here's the reason: If you put a golden egg*
>   *on them*
> *They'll get better. But not if you put a star*
>   *or moon,*
> *But the star-moon goes up*
> *And the star-moon I love.*

Hilary-Anne Farley, age 5, Canada

* * *

After every evening meal Donovan would pick up the guitar that he had left leaning against his chair and sing. The minstrel. If we took him tea in the morning the first thing he did was reach for his guitar.

At a previous meeting – a party in London given by Robert Hewison – he sat at the piano, and when asked to play 'Jennifer Juniper' he played it in a bitter minor key, full of loss. At that same party Robert Lewis spoke to Donovan out on the balcony and apparently offered to give me to him. He actually did.

I have never really known how to feel about it. So mad at Robert or mortified because Donovan turned him down. Both. I think Robert thought he loved Donovan so much he would have given him anything. Loving someone is to set her free. Or give her away and be done with her. Never mind her heart.

One evening at Seagull's Rest – after everyone had gone to bed – Robert and I sat by the last of the fire. It became clear to me that although I might not want to leave his side he was not going to be sure to stay by mine.

If I had ever been hoping for someone to look after or protect me, I knew at that moment, whether I liked it or not, that I was going to have to learn to look to myself from now on.

Property Is Theft

It was soon time to leave Seagull's Rest and move out to the wild blue yonder of the A6. It had been safe and warm in Donovan's house, even in the outbuilding where Robert and I slept, and I had no idea what the days ahead might bring. Another space to fall into, come wind come rain, over the hills to the Isle of Skye.

Saying our farewells to the friends there, we rumbled away with Bess and Blue, the wagon brightly green, red undercarriage, yellow wheels like dandelions, bucket on a hook underneath and a small sack of brown rice in the tin box that acted as our larder. We would not see nor hear from any of them again until Skye – hundreds of hoof-beaten miles away, through summer, winter and another summer, up hills and down dales, around cities and through villages, industrial towns, bleak moors, dark forests, long glens and eventually, a year later, across the sea.

We had packed the wagon carefully with only what we thought we might need out on the road, trying not to overload Bess. We left everything else we owned in a large wicker hamper in the outbuilding at Seagull's Rest, hoping one day to come back for it all.

Just a mile or so up the road I remembered I had left

something important behind, I don't know what it was, but I ran back with Blue, as Robert and Bess went on. I arrived at the door of the outbuilding to find two friends going through the hamper and picking out some of my treasured Aunt Dorothy dresses. I said nothing, picked up what I'd forgotten, turned away and ran with Blue to find the wagon, Robert, Bess, and my future.

At a party in London some years later Robert recognised his old leather jacket from that hamper on one of the guests, who was also wearing a pretty, lace-collared nightdress of mine, cut down as a shirt. Robert made him give the jacket back but I let him keep the nightie.

———

Why, How

I have little memory of those early days. Robert had the reins. We would sit up on the wagon seat if Bess was going downhill, but if uphill we would walk so as to make the wagon lighter. Mostly I walked behind with Blue, sometimes having to run to catch up if Bess broke into a trot along the flat. I had to learn the art of leaping up onto the footplate at the front of the wagon as she took off. I gave up many times, trudging after them and finding them further along the way.

We were soon joined by John James, his girlfriend Francesca

De Mayo, and Anthony McCall (another art-school friend of Robert's and John's). They had tents. Then came Scilla, who had looked Bess over before we bought her. She was a thorn in my side, showing me up many times, mostly by nimbly and successfully bounding onto the moving wagon. I knew she was thinking she would make a much better travelling companion to Robert than I did. She was most probably right.

Why did I think I was there? What was I doing, walking these long roads every day, with trucks hurtling by our tiny wagon, and my dog in danger? If anybody had asked me, I would not have known what to say. I'm just leaving London never to return, I would maybe have said. I'm going to learn how to make my own kind of life away from the madness of war and injustice – even if the madness is in me and the war has always been playing out in my head.

I was not making any kind of statement.

I was doing all that I could do at the time, in the days, in the miles going by, but it took my attention away from my troubled self and on to the problems of looking after a horse who needed water and food, a fire that needed wood, a wagon that needed a place to park every night, a dog intent on getting himself run over, and an infuriating and determined character for a partner. Finding places to stop in the urban parts of southern England was not easy since we had to have grass for Bess. Lighting a fire on the ground to boil the kettle or cook our supper was tricky in the rain, and I was quickly learning that the smoke always drifts towards the person tending the pot, making my eyes water.

* * *

Long days, finding out for myself what living without a house means. How to keep clean – difficult, but we tried, bathing in rivers and streams. How to dig a hole to shit in, how to cover it well, without being seen from the road. How to ignore the hostile stares of shopkeepers, and how to be able to laugh about being turned away from a roadside pub.

However, some of the people we met were kind and open, happy about what we were doing, interested in our story and amazed at the journey we had undertaken. Mostly they were older people. We maybe reminded them of earlier days – days they could teach us about, and we certainly listened. This was the education I felt I'd been missing. I am reminded of that journey in some way every day as there is always something to take me back, mostly gratitude for all that it changed in me. I hesitate to use the word 'healed' as it is so overused, but I did gradually find my better senses.

I do think about that time now, when I walk through my door on a cold day, dry, not scared, nor homesick, but still knowing what it is like to be homeless, to be outside and to have no shelter.

* * *

Six people had soon become just the two of us. We were the ones with the big dream, pipedream or not, and we both felt that we had to keep moving.

Just the two of us, more or less side by side, saying little, with me not really knowing if we were a couple, or just a couple of wayfarers making it up as we went along.

As Bess was trotting along one day, with us up on the wagon seat, Robert took my pretty little flowery bag of make-up and threw it over a hedge, in a high arc. We were going too fast for me to jump down, go back, find whichever hedge it was, and retrieve all my Mary Quant eyeshadow and lipstick and glowing foundation, left over from my very short-lived modelling career.

He was trying to help me adjust to my new life? Bare-faced.

'With the Dogs Eating Buttercups on the Wayside'

from 'Timothy Grub', *Just Another Diamond Day*, 1968

We gradually grew to be more aware of the great differences in people – the generous ones who would say, 'Yes, come in,' or those that wanted to call the police because the *gypsies* were coming. And we also learned a lot about the lives of Travelling people, what they went through, what they still go through. Some people would phone the village ahead and say, 'Lock up your chickens,' or call the police and say,

'Don't let them stop here.' The police would approach us and be abusive and aggressive, and then we'd start to speak, and they'd realise that we weren't Travellers, and it all completely changed. They had no idea what to make of us, or what to do with us. What were we? They were as baffled as I was. For us it turned into a game in the end – they'd say, 'What's your name?' and we'd make up names.

'Where you going?'

'Down the road.'

'Where have you come from?'

'About ten miles back that way . . .'

But there was one young copper who accepted a mug of tea and hunkered down by our fireside, shoving his hat to the back of his head. As a large black Humber car swept into the lay-by he sprang to his feet, straightening up his hat and gasping, 'Oh my God, it's the Super.' I hope he made it.

I remember clearly a small village where a gaggle of kids ran along by the side of the wagon, laughing and shouting, asking what we were doing. One little boy said, 'Can you give me a ride?' We let him clamber up onto the footplate with us and ride right through the middle of the village. At the other end his terrified father came to pull him off the wagon – he really did think we were taking his child. If that had happened to me, I would have been terrified as well – but it never occurred to me that as Travellers we could be thought to be stealing children. We were just giving his boy a ride along the street – but from then on I knew we had to be very careful. I had so much more to learn. Dogs do not eat buttercups.

* * *

We tried to do ten miles a day, but if we couldn't find a place to park up, we'd end up doing twelve, thirteen, and Bess would be getting really tired. So sometimes we would do less, and if it looked like a good place we'd stay a day or two. I got used to the heart-hammering terror of knocking on strangers' doors to ask for places to stay, but if we were lucky we would be shown to corners of fields, sometimes even given a garden to stay in for a night, or we would pull in to the side of the road if the verge was big enough and there was water nearby. Or we'd sneak into a field and be gone by morning.

We bought only the most basic of everything. I remember looking in a sweet-shop window and it was like a psychedelic vision. They were so forbidden, and we'd been living on porridge, brown rice, and onions or cabbage stolen from allotments or generous gifts of eggs or some apples from people who took us in.

I came to believe that if only I could keep moving I would find all that I needed. A belief that came to life one day when a hole appeared in my saucepan, and I found another, just by the side of the road.

Little Love Songs

Robert had once said to me 'Why don't you stop writing those miserable little love songs and write about what is around you?' So I did. In a way it was the end of my own songwriting, about my own self and feelings. Me. Was he right? I will never know.

Apart from the love song that was 'Glow Worms' (about him), my songs became narratives. I think 'Timothy Grub' was probably the first, because that was the story of being in the wood and being thrown out and finding the horse and wagon. (Timothy Grub was Robert, Emily Grub was me, and Maurice Snail was John James.)

Much later Robert wrote the words to three songs – 'Window Over the Bay', 'Hebridean Sun' and 'Trawlerman's Song' – and I think it's often not acknowledged that he was very much the author of the whole endeavour. It was his idea to get on the road with a horse, and although we came to it together and the whole journey happened for both of us, it was originally his vision.

John James has said recently that there were a lot of people like us doing the same thing at that time, that we were not special. But they were not like us. Robert had been inspired by some young aristocrats he had known – with their beautiful Romany wagons and horses, flowing robes and a mission to travel the length of ley lines all the way to Glastonbury Tor – but they were not penniless like we were.

Nor were they heading out for a different life hundreds of miles away at the other end of the British Isles in an old bread van. They had homes to go back to.

We were special, by any reading of the word, always and forever.

Rubbish Tip

Approaching the town of Derby, we had a choice to make. It was already getting quite late in the day and we needed somewhere to stop – a verge, a field – anywhere we could find grass, water and wood. We had to quickly decide whether to carry on through the town or take the bypass around it. Thinking there might be more chance of finding a place to draw the wagon onto we took the bypass. Big mistake. Miles and miles of suburban houses, no verges, no grass anywhere.

Bess was getting too tired so we took a turning off the main road, past the Rolls-Royce factory. Behind the factory was a rubbish tip. We had to stop there as the chance of finding anything better was waning with the day.

I remember it as mountainous piles of broken wood and fence posts, tangled wire and bald tyres, fridges and sacking and bent-up rusting iron – as far as the eye could see.

Whilst we unharnessed Bess and found her a few clumps of grass we realised we were getting stared at. Little eyes above the wreckage, tiny laughter and shy advance. These five children lived with their parents in a caravan parked on the edge of the tip. The whole family walked across to introduce themselves and we realised that the travelling community already knew all about us. Their systems of communication far outdid those of the police.

We were pitied for our very small wagon and the offer was made to there and then take the top off and build a decent living space onto the base, big enough for a stove and a proper bed. 'Won't take long,' they said. It was so tempting, but we were fond of our old bread van with its oval windows, shaped canopy and sheet-metal covered sides.

Kindness continued with the family going to the fish and chip shop and bringing us our supper. This was so very welcome as I had just boiled our kettle on some rough wood – wood that had probably been impregnated with some kind of bitumen preservative – and the tea tasted poisonous. Their bottle of lemonade tasted heavenly. We spent the evening listening to stories, told with a humour I would come to know as that of a people who understand too much of oppression and hatred.

Next morning was a Sunday, and as we harnessed Bess up again and went to say grateful goodbyes to our generous hosts, their perfectly Sunday-dressed children lined up and waved us off. Ribbons and bows, white lace frocks – and the boys with slick hair and bow ties.

I was reluctant to leave them.

The Right Track

The next clear recollections are from the time we came near to Leek, in Staffordshire, to where my father's sister and my uncle the GP lived. The uncle who had introduced me to ley lines and prehistory and all the things over which I thought he and Robert would enjoy finding common ground.

We were looking for the old track to a small farm that my Grandpa Bunyan had bought when he retired after the war. It was called Roughstone Hall. It sounded grand but it was a small stone-built cottage. When my father's younger brother Jim was demobbed from the war, he helped to build up the farm with a new cowshed and a barn for the hay. My first memories are of the enormous backsides of the cows, the collecting of bantam eggs and the warm safety of the kitchen where Grandma Bunyan baked bread in the big black cast-iron cooking range, and churned the butter. I always imagined this was her way of life, only later realising that she was recreating scenes from her own childhood – as I would go on to do from these moments in mine.

* * *

Roughstone Hall was up and down a long track, over a ford and through a large field with a brook running through it. It had stone mullioned windows, and a rickety wooden staircase to the loft where as a young child I would be put to bed behind a curtain.

Finding the end of the track so many years later with Robert and Bess in 1968 felt to me almost like finding home. We stopped in the big field and started to unharness Bess. As her bridle and collar came off and before we got the chance to put on her halter she made off – back up the track to the main road – with Robert hot on her heels waving his arms and yelling at her to stop. She had never done this before, never made such a bid for freedom. As they reached the road she continued on down the white line at a speed Robert could not match. He tells how he flagged down a truck, jumped in and shouted, *'FOLLOW THAT HORSE!'*.

About a mile down the road Bess suddenly veered off into the garden of a small house, where she set about coolly grazing the lawn. As Robert approached her, she looked up at him and quietly lowered her head into the halter.

She never did it again; maybe she didn't need to. She'd had her say.

* * *

Grandpa and Grandma Bunyan were long gone. A mother and daughter who took in stray dogs now had the cottage. The two had lived in Leek town but their neighbours had complained about the barking and so they bought Roughstone Hall with its large cowshed – the one built by my Uncle Jim – and housed all their beloved rescued dogs in kennels there. The happiest of people. I will never forget their kindness and acceptance of our ways. They understood disapproval just as well as we did. We helped to feed the dogs, though all they had to give them was stale bread donated by the bakers, mixed in with gravy powder and hot water.

I wrote 'Rainbow River' in their field – and sang it to them verse by verse, evening by evening, as the words came to me. The cottage was transformed, the mullioned windows gone, the old black cast-iron cooking range replaced by a modern stone fireplace with brass ornaments across the mantelpiece. Each one was imprinted on my mind as I sang.

The rainbow river is a laughing stream
Down in a valley by a mountain that is pine-tree tall
The rainbow river has a small boy fishing with a worm
And a jam jar by the waterfall
Don't make a sound, don't disturb the ground
The biggest fish you ever saw is around
And the rainbow river gives a rainbow fish
As one small boy goes running quietly to his mother's call

The stone-built farmhouse is a rough stone cottage
Hiding close against the hillside up a winding track
The stone-built farmhouse has a fair-haired farmer
Wearing wooden shoes and building up a new haystack
Run in the door, stand on the stone floor
The oven opens – there's the biggest loaf you ever saw
And the stone-built farmhouse gives a good warm welcome
As he sits down in his own chair with a Windsor back

The magpie meadow is a glowing evening colour
Sun is setting quietly and the boy is tired
The magpie meadow has a sparrowhawk who hovers
Hanging on the wind, preying eagle eyed
Sit by the lantern, watch as the years turn
Slowly bringing truth for every child to learn

And the magpie meadow darkens gently blue now
As the family sit, their faces lit by ember fire

'Rainbow River', *Just Another Diamond Day*, 1968

* * *

My aunt and my uncle the GP had invited us to come for lunch at their house in Leek, Regent House. That morning we bathed and washed our hair in the cold water of the brook, got out all our best clothes and dressed in what we thought would be suitable visiting finery. Robert in red velvet trousers, a golden shirt with raised green patterns, and a green silk neckerchief. I wore a long black skirt with golden stars, a white lacy Victorian blouse and a black silk cut-velvet waistcoat. We felt pretty fine.

As my aunt opened the door of Regent House, she didn't even look at us but said 'I've run the bath for you' – pointing the way up the stairs.

This widened the rift between some of my relatives and Robert that never really healed. Where I had thought my uncle and Robert would have a shared interest with stories of ley lines and the magic of ancient history, I was quite wrong. We were lectured about our direly irresponsible behaviour. We were given notepaper and envelopes to write to our respective parents and told we were *'Not quite drawing room'* for living together unmarried under the same roof –albeit an old six-foot by three-foot horse-drawn bread wagon.

These people I had idolised dearly all my life suddenly seemed to be alien. I'm sure they were only concerned for me – after all, they had looked after me so well and kindly the year before and tried to get me on to what they would have thought was an even keel. To have me show up on their doorstep looking like I did – 'a tramp!' apparently, must have hurt their respectable feelings deeply.

That generation, who felt (and reminded us often) they had been through terrible wars and deprivation and made enormous sacrifices so that we could have the lives they hadn't been able to live – surely would have found it impossible to accept our rejection of their ways. I understood it and loved them still, but Robert was terminally humiliated by people he had only just met. He never forgave them.

My father's younger brother Jim – the one who had helped my grandparents build up the farm at Roughstone Hall – still lived nearby, and had a small builder's yard. We paid him and his wife Agnes a visit before heading back to the wagon. My dear Uncle Jim chuckled, his round-spectacled and round pink-cheeked smiling face gave me great courage as he said, 'It's all freedom, isn't it, Vash?'

The contrast between the chilly reproach of Regent House and the warmth of Uncle Jim and Auntie Aggie's tin teapot on the hearth made me quite and completely certain I was on the right road.

Rags and Bones

Carnforth, Lancashire. Getting along on the flat, Bess walking, with us sitting up on the wagon, mostly sunny, contentedly peaceful between us.

Suddenly we were overtaken by a high-trotting horse and rattling two-wheeled spring cart driven by a widely grinning, waving man beckoning us to follow him. As he swerved off the road into a fenced yard, we realised he was a rag-and-bone man, or scrap merchant. He was also a smallholder with pigs in a pen and chickens around the yard. Just back from his day collecting anything unwanted by anybody, door-to-door around the streets, he cheerfully asked us about ourselves and laughed at us for what we were doing.

He invited me to look through his most recent hoard which he had just tipped out onto the ground from hessian sacks – and said to take whatever I wanted. His wife came out of the house and scowled at me, but he waved her away. I should have bowed to her superiority and let her go through everything first, but I had not learned that kind of grace as yet.

Crisp white linen lace-edged sheets and pillowcases. White Victorian nightdress. An eiderdown quilt, pink and silky. White collarless shirts for Robert. I could have gathered much more but we were always aware of the weight on Bess, which was why we left possessions here and there along the way, intending to go back and collect them one day. We never did.

I made up the wagon bed with the lace-edged sheets folded down over the eiderdown with the lacy pillows placed straight and perfect, ready for the night.

Invited into the house for supper, I had to try not to gaze on the many chocolate biscuits lying brightly in their silver wrappers on the table, and to wait until they were offered. I sang a few songs as I always did for anyone who took us in; we said our goodnights and thank yous and looked forward to climbing into our clean pink and white bed.

My Blue had got there first, after a rolling visit to the pigpen.

*   *   *

One day later we were flagged down by a man at the side of the road. He asked if we needed somewhere to stay the night, which we did by that time, and he led us up a track onto a hill overlooking the surrounding landscape 360 degrees, where he told us to help ourselves to wood and water and make ourselves at home. So, for two days running we did not have to knock on any doors or plead, nor tie Bess up at the side of the A6. Two safe places in a row.

As dusk fell there appeared a vision out of the mist, a man on a white horse with flowing mane. It was our generous landowner, who turned out to be the sheriff of Westmorland.

When invited to his house the next day he pointed to a small framed black and white photograph on the wall by the fireplace. It was of him and his wife on their honeymoon, with a pony and two-wheeled spring cart, with hoops and a canvas over the top. We had reminded him of younger times.

Lakes

The Lake District, the first wildly beautiful place we had come across. We strayed from the A6 in order to visit an art-school friend of Robert's whose parents had a house in a small village called Nibthwaite. We parked the wagon, and Bess, in a neighbouring farmer's field. I remember overstaying our welcome as I had had to return south for a few days to visit my increasingly ill mother, so by the time I rejoined Robert we were well into September. It was getting to that point in the year when farmers become anxious about how much grass is left, and are not so generous with allowing vagrant travellers to graze a horse in their fields.

'Are you one of them students?'

'No.'

'Well what are you then?'

How could we answer that?

So, we left to find somewhere else to stay. We found the perfect place, directly opposite Nibthwaite, the other side of Lake Coniston on some common ground, in amongst the gorse bushes. Robert had work with a couple in a big house over the lake and they allowed him to use their boat to go back and forth. He painted their windows and dug the garden whist I stayed with the horse and the dog, and rode Bess to collect the milk from the nearest farm with a small tin churn. I built a fireplace with stones and kept the ground around it swept with a broom I had made from the broom shrubs that also grew close by. I sewed and embroidered with the little pieces of cloth and silks that the woman Robert worked for had kindly given to me, and started to make patchwork curtains for the wagon. Roughly.

I had a large zinc tub for washing the clothes, which I mostly boiled up with soap over the fire and then rinsed out in the lake. I had long since been taught by a Traveller woman to use the thorn bushes to drape and dry things on, in the sun and the wind, carefully.

I always knew when Robert was coming back because Blue would suddenly leap up and run down to the shore, hearing the oars on the water long before I could.

I cooked horrible meals on the open fire mostly made of lentils, cabbage and potatoes. Food tastes better outside – thankfully. I was constantly hungry, wanted chocolate and missed my mother. I started to try to make bread, pies, anything that remotely looked like the dishes she made. I buried an old black cast-iron pot in the embers and covered the lid with more embers to try to make an oven. I made pastry out of brown flour and Echo margarine, pressing the dough onto a plate as I had no rolling pin or flat surface. I peeled the dough off the plate and lay it over a dish full of, yes, lentils, cabbage and potatoes. And onions. I cut leaf-shaped pieces of dough and laid them around the centre of the pie plate which I carefully laid on little stones in the iron pot. Yes, I burned it.

I learned after a while to put water in the bottom of the pot, just enough so that by the time it had boiled away the pie or bread would be cooked, and then the piled-up embers would have just long enough to brown and not blacken it. Meals improved.

Since we were staying in one place for a while, we decided we should try to get Bess in foal. The farm where I got the milk had a thoroughbred stallion so we took Bess along one day when we thought she was in season. As we walked her into the yard, we heard a wailing of hair-freezing eeriness. In the middle of the cobbled yard was a dog, a black, matted, skinny dog, tied up, with its back to us and its eyes tight shut and long snout howling up at the sky.

We asked the farmer how much it would be to have Bess served by his stallion and he said, 'Five pounds and take that bloody dog with you.'

Bess had an afternoon with the stallion and we happily took her and the dog back to the wagon. It was an Afghan Hound underneath it all. Her story was that she had been kept for breeding as her puppies would be valuable, but she had never had any company, dog or human. She had been kept in a room for all of her two years but had produced no puppies. It had never occurred to her owners that she might be too distressed to conceive. The farmer had taken her out of pity, but she was afraid – away from her room for the first time and around people – she didn't know where she was and so she cried.

He warned us to keep her tied up at all times. We tied her to the wagon and called her Magog, shortened to May. She was completely unable to respond. She looked about her all the time, like a hawk – red eyes, expressionless. Her ears didn't move when we spoke to her, she didn't even flinch when we stroked her and tried to untangle her hair. Nothing. So, we spoke and stroked and treated her much like Blue, who was fascinated by her but she even ignored him.

For two weeks she stayed the same until one day I was leaning over the fire, poking the boiling soapy clothes with a stick, when I felt a paw on my back. I turned around and she was looking at me. I don't think May ever wagged her tail in the time we had her, but sometimes the end of it twitched and this is what it did as she looked at me for the first time.

Robert set about trying to train her but it was going to be another long road.

White Black Horse

Bess was on a long chain tether and collar all the days we stayed on the shore of Lake Coniston as there were no fences. We would move her around so she had fresh grazing every day, and water in buckets from the lake.

One quiet night we both heard the sound of hoof beats and looked out of the wagon to see that Bess was off her tether, away in a small clearing amongst the gorse bushes, glowing pale in the mist. Robert went one way around the road and I went the other through the gorse, so that we could each walk towards her and catch her.

As we met in the clearing all we could make out was each other. She had disappeared between us. Wide-eyed and spooked we went back to the wagon to find Bess quietly standing, still on her tether, nodding sleepily in the night air.

I liked to imagine she had been astrally projecting herself away into a place with no collar and chain, no harness, no pulling our house uphill – a white apparition free to trick us and get us to jump out of our lazy beds. I hoped she was enjoying her starry trip.

Kindness

We stayed there on the common a few weeks until we had to go away south again for a short visit, now with two dogs. We found a field where we could leave Bess and the wagon for the days we were away. My mother was no better and was sent to live with and be nursed by my GP uncle and aunt in Leek as I could not stay. A caustic regret that would stay with me.

This time we came back to Bess with John James in his old Austin, Happiness Runs – with a dulcitone in the back which I sat on. This was a small portable keyboard in a mahogany case with fold-up legs. They were made at the end of the nineteenth century for missionaries to carry around with them, the hammers hitting tuning forks so they never went out of tune whatever climate they endured, always sounding like a celeste. It had belonged to my brother's wife, as had the small Spanish guitar of her grandmother's that I had taken with me on the journey.

We got back to the boathouse where we had stored our belongings to find the guitar that my sister-in-law had lent me fatally dampened and sprung to pieces. I had not thought to loosen the strings. Unforgivable.

It was becoming autumnal and wet, cold even by now. No stove in the wagon, nowhere to dry our clothes, shivering dogs.

We heard of a caravan park where we might be able to

rent something with a stove in it. We went off in Happiness Runs but could not find it, so stopped to ask directions from a white-haired man standing at the side of the road. He told us the way, looked at us, looked at the car and then asked what were we doing and why. Robert told him about our stalled journey to Skye, and he said, 'We are leaving tomorrow for the Outer Hebrides – you'd better come in and have a cup of tea and meet my wife.'

So, we did. Me in the long brown tweedy dress that I had inherited from my sister-in-law's very large grandmother – the artist Grace Wheatley – and wellington boots, all of us equally dishevelled and worn having been outside for days.

Mac and Iris Macfarlane lived in a beautiful old Lakeland house called Field Head. They had recently bought a ruined croft house and some land on North Uist in the Outer Hebridean islands, beyond Skye, and were packing their car full of the things they thought they would need for the winter there. They were going to live in the one side of the house that still had a roof, the other side having a tree in it.

Within fifteen minutes they had offered us their warm, dry, Aga-heated house, with soft beds and dry floors and a bathroom, to look after till their return in the spring. They were wondering whether they had room to take the potato masher.

They gave us the keys and left for their dream house in the northerly gales, whilst we went to collect Bess and the wagon to bring them to our windfall of a winter roof, and a farmer's kind offer to keep our horse in his field opposite the house.

* * *

Bess hauled the wagon up and down the hills towards Field Head. As we let her rest at a crossroads a young couple approached us and asked if we knew the way to the Drunken Duck pub. We didn't, but passed the resting time in conversation with them. They were from southern Holland and on their honeymoon. As we were on our way to our first night in Mac and Iris's house, we invited them to come to supper.

As usual after the meal Robert brought me my guitar and I sang. It was my job – as it had been Donovan's – to sing to the people who had eaten with us. He had been the minstrel, always ready to pick up his own guitar that was constantly at his side. I had to be cajoled. I was shy, I was not a performer, but Robert so wanted me to be like Donovan.

So, I sang to the Dutch couple, and they invited us to go to Holland at Christmas. I wasn't sure – my mother so ill and me increasingly troubled for leaving her. They suggested we do some concerts whilst there; he was a journalist – he could fix them up. We had almost no money, in fact John was the only one of us who had anything much at all. It seemed like a good chance for me to earn something.

A while later we received boat tickets from them for Rotterdam, and a promise of a series of shows. He was to be my agent for the tour.

Catch One Leaf

But it was still November – *autumn I'll remember*. The Aga stove was old, battered and temperamental, but the radiant warmth of it gradually dried out my bones. I cooked just about edible meals on it but at least they didn't taste of smoke. I had a real oven at last and tried my hand at cakes. Solid brown cakes. I used custard powder and brown sugar for icing. Even I couldn't eat it.

I walked to Hawkshead and bought food at the Co-op store. Echo margarine was sevenpence ha'penny for a half pound. I smiled at people who looked startled by my appearance and who didn't ever smile back in all the days that I walked down to do my shopping there.

The cobbler was better in that at least he talked to us.

Robert already had lace-up clogs, which he took in for repair – and I asked for a pair of red ones to be made for me. Whilst he nailed the irons like horseshoes onto wooden soles the cobbler told tales of Beatrix Potter and said she'd been a mean old woman who brought in one clog at a time to be mended. He said she never smiled. Maybe the Co-op ladies were related to her.

Walking back from Hawkshead the hedgerows were full of rose hips. At the house I sat on a window seat and watched the leaves being blown about and the trees bending and thanked the sky that I was indoors. I felt blessed, which of course I was. What had made Mac and Iris trust us? I have never asked. They knew nothing about us but maybe recognised kindred in the madness of what we were all doing. Whatever their reasoning, their kindness saved us from a bleak midwinter.

'Rose Hip November' and 'Swallow Song' were written sitting on that window seat. Months of walking the road and living on the ground had given me a way of looking at the world around me which from here might seem childlike, I do know that.

It wasn't that the hills and road and trees became like people in my head, but more that I felt no different to them and saw them all as living and being, possessing some kind of relation to each other – and to me.

Outside I had become a part of my surroundings rather than a player within them. That beetles should have as much of a right to be here as I do had always been obvious to me, but actually living in the same place as them had an effect. It made me hesitate, move them carefully from where I wanted to sit down.

*   *   *

I had grown up in the city, visiting relatives' farms in holidays and getting the idea that it was all about lambs, and hay bales, and combine harvesters. Like the illustrations in a child's farmyard book, I only watched and was beguiled. But through the journey I began to understand what farms were for.

As I walked up the A6 pondering on the cows curling their tongues round the grass, and the sheep delicately taking their small bites, I had to put it all in place. The landscape only being as it was because of the sheep and the cows. The calves and lambs born to be slaughtered if male, allowed to live and reproduce if female. The calves removed from their mothers and the noise of them through the first night and the resigned silence of the second. The cutting off of the lambs' tails and the slicing off of their tiny testicles. The bulls in dark sheds with furious red eyes and revenge in mind. The yelling and clattering of sticks on slow bony backsides as the cattle are pressed into trucks. The plain raw killing.

Everything seemed suddenly unbearably stolen.

Saddened and wised up to the brutality of it all I still ached for the long-gone, warm heart of Grandma Bunyan's farm kitchen, her stove and her bread. There I had not had a thought for the plight of the beasts outside, just a neat enjoyment of the butter she churned. Sitting on the window seat in Mac and Iris's house I made the ache into the words of the songs.

The life, the innocence I longed for.

Catch one leaf and fortune will surround you evermore

'Rose Hip November',
Just Another Diamond Day, 1968

———

Vlissingen

Christmas was coming. My first away from my family but my mother was in Leek with my aunt and uncle, and I could not be going there with Robert. We decided we would take up the offer of a Dutch tour. I wrote a long, illustrated letter to my mother and gave it to a friend to post for me – forgetting to ask her to put a first class stamp on it to get it there in time for Christmas. Second class – it did not get there in time. She didn't know I wasn't there, but I did.

We took a train to Hull and the boat to Rotterdam. The young couple who had invited us, and planned a tour for me, lived in a very new house in a modern town. So strange to be in these airless rooms after the draughty familiarity of Mac and Iris's Field Head.

Our first date was a youth club. Young faces stared, bewildered, in a room decorated with balloons and welcome streamers.

Bewilderment continued, within me as well, not knowing how I came to be singing to children in a language they would not understand. At one show, again playing to children, I must have seemed so despondent that Robert got up and stood beside me to sing Donovan's song 'Happiness Runs' with a false gaiety which made me retreat even further.

Christmas Day came and went unmarked, uncelebrated by our Dutch hosts. We had no money for presents for each other – or for them – though they would have been quite puzzled to receive any. When I asked when we might get any fees, I was told there was no profit as yet since they had paid for our boat tickets, and also the taxi fares to the venues.

I embroidered a piece of velvet ribbon with *I love you*, rolled it up and fixed it with a small pearl button. I had a tiny silver bucket with me that my brother had made in our father's dental laboratory when I was ten – first carving it out of pink wax and then casting it with silver from a melted-down two-shilling piece as I watched, enchanted. (Another trick he showed me at the time was to silver a copper penny in the plating tank. I took it to the sweet shop hoping to pass it off as a half-crown. Luckily it was returned to me with just a raised eyebrow.)

So, in Holland for Christmas day, I sewed up a small

envelope from a scrap of velvet, put in the ribbon, the silver bucket, a farthing coin with a robin on it, and a small shard of pottery. That was Robert's first Christmas present from me. I still have it.

* * *

My next singing date was in a bar in Ghent, Belgium, where we were sent by train, unaccompanied by our agent. After three songs sung against the glass clinks and chatter and loud ignoring of my presence, I burst into tears and ran off the stage. The barman was a kind man, handed me my fee anyway, and told us to go upstairs where we would find a musician who lived in some rooms above the bar.

It was Derroll Adams, the banjo player, who had played with Ramblin' Jack Elliott in days past and had been a great mentor to Donovan. The last time I'd seen him was at Donovan's house, Seagull's Rest, where he had arrived in the middle of one night, been unable to raise anyone and so had slept curled up on the doormat in the front porch.

Here in Ghent, he had apparently had a heart attack and was recovering. He understood my shyness and distress at being unheard, but how I expected shyness and a quiet voice to be noticed in any way I do not know. I don't really think I did. I was just doing it to earn some money and to please Robert who so very much wanted me to be a Star, rather than the very non-star that I was.

There was a banjo lying in an open case – Robert picked

it up and placed it into Derroll's unwilling arms. He said he would play if I would sing, so of course I agreed. The shower of silvery notes was entrancing, his stiff hands coming to life, and then he smiled expectantly at me. I don't recall which song I sang but he said something that would change my life forever.

'Don't Hide Your Light.'

* * *

What we did next was not good. We had the fee from the bar in Ghent and so we went to the train station, bought tickets for Rotterdam and the ferry back to Hull, and from there a train to London. We were stealing away, away from the pain, for me, of singing to people who did not want to or couldn't hear – and from the two people who had brought us there with the promise of a tour, which turned out to be a lot less than we'd believed it would be. It is a sad memory for me as I don't think there was any real fault on anyone's part, but high expectations that were not lived up to, by any of us.

But another thing that would change my life happened on that train back through Belgium. The flat, neat fields ploughed by fat, short-legged horses, the haystacks in perfect rows, the seeds being sown.

I felt I could be happy with that. A blade of grass, a grain of wheat – and a word.

So, it became:

Just another diamond day
Just a blade of grass
Just another bale of hay
And the horses pass.

Just another field to plough
Just a grain of wheat
Just a sack of seed to sow
And the children eat.

Just another life to live
Just a word to say
Just another love to give
And a diamond day

'Diamond Day', *Just Another Diamond Day*, 1968

* * *

We had a day in London before heading back to Bess and the wagon and Field Head in the Lake District. We stayed the night with a friend of Robert's – Christopher Sykes – who had been at Ravensbourne College with Robert and John. He knew Joe Boyd.

I knew of Joe but had never met him – although he had tried to get me to go to see him two years earlier, after he had seen me singing at the poetry reading in the ICA. In the same way that the poetry of that evening had gone over my airy head, I had dismissed the idea of going to meet an

American who I imagined to be a big old guy behind a large desk smoking a cigar, and anyway at that time I was more inclined to accept Tony Calder's invitation to go back to record for Immediate.

Idiot. When I did finally go to see him two years later at Christopher's suggestion, Joe turned out to be young, tall, blondly beautiful – no cigar.

I told him what I was doing, played him some songs, probably 'Rose Hip November' and my newest song 'Diamond Day'.

He had wanted to make an album with me all that time before when I had stupidly ignored him – but now he said he'd like to record these new songs as a document of the journey, once we had completed it and reached Donovan's islands. I had vowed never to set foot in a recording studio again ever, but Derroll Adams's words rang in my ears and so I agreed.

Joe gave me what I remember as five pounds but what Robert remembers as thirty, a copy of the Incredible String Band's *Wee Tam and the Big Huge* (a double vinyl) and an invitation to dinner, with him and the band, that night.

I had no idea who they were, but Robert knew.

We all sat on cushions at low tables in a basement, a Moroccan restaurant in Kings Road. They were dressed in Eastern finery and I was in my old brown tweed dress and a pair of worn brown brogues I had found in a cupboard. I said not a word all night.

* * *

Mum died. 'Mothers do.' I miss her to this day.

My mother would dance sometimes
Believing herself alone
But through a slightly open door
I would watch her as she turned,
Turned round, round
Briefly unbound

My mother played and sang sometimes
Believing herself alone
But through a slightly open door
I could see her face upturned
Songs long learned
So long untuned

I was her only audience
She believed herself alone
My applause should have been rapturous
But I closed the door
And turned, turned away

'Mother', *Heartleap*, 2011

———

Cumbria

Back to Hawkshead – in the middle of maybe the prettiest part of the Lake District. These days it is painted white and the cobbler's is a teashop and it is full of people wanting to see where Beatrix Potter lived. When I was there that winter of 1968 into '69 it was a dour, damp place, the houses grey lime-washed – a small country town surrounded by working farms.

Robert and John met an old man in the pub who seemingly went there on his ancient pony every night, then at the end of the evening was put back onto his pony, who took him home. He fell off onto his doorstep and the pony put itself to bed. He was an old horseman and so was a well of information for Robert, who went to work for him occasionally. His farm was terminally chaotic and so the work was erratic, but whilst I was back in the house making terrible cakes Robert was learning about the mysteries of horse-whispering, the Horseman's Word, and hearing some good stories of days gone by.

Our immediate neighbour was a more efficient farmer and when May the Afghan got off her tether one day and chased a herd of his bullocks down the hill where they charged straight through a fence, taking a good hundred feet of it with them, he threatened Robert with a sickle and punched his ear.

Robert and John were out on a lake one day with the dogs in a small rowing boat. May jumped out and swam to the shore and by time they caught up with her – rowing frantically – she had a chicken in her mouth. That was our Magog, shortened to May. I so well remember the shape of that beautiful hound, one of the many times she escaped, running as if for her life over the snow-covered hills, trailing the long horse's rein that had been keeping her tied up. A true running dog for sure, if only we could let her.

She came into season and all of the neighbourhood dogs queued up by the front door. Dear silly Blue knew not what to do. The postman fought his way through them to deliver a letter to the 'Beautiful People'. I frowned when he gave it to me, but he couldn't know that I didn't think of myself as one of them and he made me shudder with his leery comment about free love.

Robert sold an antique copper gunpowder flask to a local dealer. This dealer gave John a small panel of ancient-looking wood and asked him to paint an icon – providing him with the gold leaf he would need. It looked the part, of course; John could and did turn his hand to anything, especially painting.

John James. Sometimes he would sleep on the kitchen table so he wouldn't have to get up for breakfast. I put his words for 'Where I Like to Stand' to a tune that was in my head.

I think it was February when Joe Boyd came up for a visit. I cooked lentil stew and baked potatoes. No cakes. I wore a peasanty blouse and long black velvet skirt and my new, blistering red clogs. It was good to see him, and to show him the beautiful landscapes around where we were living.

There was never any chance of our staying in Cumbria; our path was to Skye and the promise there, but I had fallen for the gentle hills and Herdwick sheep and the farm kitchens that must have been burned into my young mind through Beatrix Potter drawings – here it was in reality. I baked and swept and cleaned and washed the clothes. I loved the picture of the stove and the pulley hanging from the ceiling – full of clean pillowcases and shirts, but occasionally it did occur to me that it was not quite fair that all the chores fell to me.

Robert told me I was lucky that I had a job.

'Come Wind, Come Rain, We're off Again'

from 'Come Wind Come Rain', *Just Another Diamond Day*,
1970

Just after my twenty-fourth birthday. The lighter days meant
we should be on our way again. My mother no longer needing my remorse at having left her – since she had now left
me for good – I could return to the big idea of getting us
away to Skye.

I had finished the patchwork curtains for the wagon,
John and Robert had built doors for the back and put
a wooden floor in at the height of the front seat for the
mattress to lay on, with space for all our belongings underneath. The red and white striped awning was now hung
from hooks all the way around the front canopy, and so
now we could stretch out the full length of the wagon
instead of having our feet sticking out of the back. The
front part of the mattress was bent back in the daytime,
kept in place by a leather strap the width of the wagon,
making a back for the seat.

The same Traveller woman who had long before
instructed me to dry the washing by draping it on thorn
bushes had also told me to have everything in bags, not
boxes. Boxes were for gadgies, anyone who was not a Traveller, she said. A lot more could be packed into a small space
in bags.

John went back to London. Iris was back from Uist

and waved Robert and me, Bess, Blue and May away. As we rumbled down the road I felt a strange regret for leaving the known and loved for the unknown and faraway north.

I wore my mother's pink and white spotted apron. I tied it around my waist for a very long time, as a piece of her that I was able to take with me – that and her platinum wedding ring, which has not left my hand since, although now thinner and slightly buckled.

The weather was kindly, the sun was gleaming with a mother-of-pearl light. Walking alongside Bess I looked back at those low misty Lakeland hills and wondered if I would ever see them again.

We stopped to rest Bess and boil up the kettle for tea at the side of the road. Green shoots and a gentle breeze settled my heart and gave me reason to keep going. The rock I sat on had been warmed by the midday sun.

A little spring spider walks over my knee.

For two days we walked and celebrated the early spring, loving our freedom from the four stone walls, until on the third day the heavens opened and soaked our bones.

Robert's cloak was heavy with rain and dripped all around its hem; I had nothing waterproof, and Bess had steam rising from her back with streams of water running off her flanks. There were not many buildings around as we were still in the Cumbrian hills, but we headed for a farmhouse up a track.

The woman who opened the door didn't even ask what we wanted, laughed, put on her coat and hat, came out into the rain and led us to a barn where she gave us hay, and some straw to rub Bess down with. She brought her some water and a bucket of oats, told us to change our wet clothes and she would dry them for us. She said that when we had settled the horse we must come into the house where she had been preparing supper for her large family. There would be plenty for us.

I wish I had asked her more about herself, but my abiding picture of her is from the next day when the sun shone again and there was a warm wind. She was pegging washing to a line on a hill, against the sky, big basketsful of washing – and she was singing.

I wanted to be her.

Borders

The road flattened out towards Carlisle, and on towards the Scottish border. By now we had come to tag the 'no' people and the 'yes' people – those who wouldn't even open their doors to us, and those who opened them wide.

It seemed to us that sometimes we would hit a seam of 'no' people, as if it were contagious from one neighbour to another. And then there would be a sunnier stretch of days where we would find acceptance, interest, laughter and a gift of maybe a bale of hay or some oats.

By the time we had crossed the border into Scotland – past Gretna and on to Annan – I was getting the feeling I was in another country. And so I was. In Annan a coalman with a horse and long black cart stopped to speak to us, curious as to what we were doing there. I could not tell if he was friendly or not. He looked at me and asked if I was left- or right-footed. I looked at my shoes. At least it made him laugh as he had meant was I Catholic or Protestant.

I don't know what he made of us, but it was my first lesson in knowing that I was English. It hadn't crossed my southern mind before that there was a difference.

Golden Virginia and Wonders

Stopping at a farm in Ayrshire, I remember rain, being cold and mournful – and the kind farmer who gave me some Golden Virginia tobacco and a packet of papers to cheer me up. It was about as good as I remembered as I hadn't been able to smoke at all throughout the whole journey. Robert disliked smokers and anyway there was only enough money for food and blacksmiths. I made the thinnest of roll-ups and eked out that tobacco for as long as I could, keeping it in a small bag and guarding it most carefully in case Robert were to throw it over a hedge.

This farmer grew potatoes – he called them Golden Wonders. They were golden indeed, and bright yellow all the way through. He gave us plenty, and some butter, and for sure they were the best I had ever tasted. He was proud of them and said, 'You won't need no beef' – and he was right.

I had a book where I wrote down all the addresses of the many good, kind-hearted and interesting people that we met along the way, with notes about them. I planned to let them all know once we had arrived at our destination. I lost it.

One child I remember well was a boy at a jockey training school near the Erskine Bridge. Robert and I were staying at the farm next door, having been given a job painting all the doors of the barns and outhouses in traditional green. This little jockey was maybe about eleven or twelve. He befriended us and showed me where the horses' feed was kept in a shed, with great tubs of bran, oats and a large vat as big as an oil drum full of honey.

I understood this boy as he seemed to understand me, and we laughed a lot. We were both a long way away from home and family, deprived of sweetness. He was a little overweight for a jockey and I was growing by the day with the porridge I cooked every morning, porridge that I ate until I hurt and the tops of my wellington boots came to be tight around my legs.

The honey for the racehorses was dark, thick and slightly crunchy, and no honey I have ever tasted since could match it. I couldn't stay away from it and neither could he.

I didn't want to leave him – or the honey – but leave we had to once all the doors were done. We were paid for the painting and also given a brass jam pan that was in one of the outhouses. Given. We did not steal it. I just stole honey from next door.

Cats and Dogs and Otters

We came to the Milton Cat and Dog Home where we asked for a place to stay the night. We were looked after like the strays that the owner took in. She was fierce and strong, and she must have liked us as she surely rescued us when we were further up the road. Someone had given us a haggis and I cooked it on a fire on the shore of Loch Lomond. Next day Robert was very ill. I went to a phone box and called the owner at the cat and dog home (whose name I cannot remember now as it was in the book that I lost) and after I'd found a field where I could leave Bess and the wagon safely for a few days, she came to collect us in her car.

She was a friend of Gavin Maxwell, the writer of *Ring of Bright Water* – the classic story of a man with his pet otters, living on a remote part of the Scottish west coast, inaccessible except by boat. We read the book whilst Robert was recovering and it sealed all that we'd ever dreamed of in our vision of a faraway island life. *Tarka the Otter* had figured largely in my childhood as maybe the only book I actually listened to and learned from, loved and cried about, when I was ten or eleven, so these more recent stories of otters and wilderness and wild sea were just what I needed to keep me going.

With Robert getting better, on we went, with a key to a cottage we would not reach for many miles. It would be in Glenelg, just before a sea-crossing to Skye, a cottage belonging to Gavin Maxwell which might be empty, a possible roof to look forward to.

But for now, back to the shores of Loch Lomond which I remember for being unfriendly. No one would let us stop in fields or any piece of ground. Much of it belonged to the Colquhoun estate whose employees seemed too scared to lose their tied houses if they were to displease the laird. At least they were honest enough to say we weren't worth the risk.

At times like this Bess would be tied up with her chain and collar wherever we could get the wagon off the road.

Remembering exactly what happened when and where is difficult for this bit of the journey. When I look at the map it's hard to believe we did it. Forestry Commission land for miles and miles, impenetrable pine trees so close to each other that nothing could grow underneath them. Sunlight did not reach the ground. Or the road.

I'm not sure whereabouts we were but Robert became very ill again. We found our way to a doctor, an elderly woman who phoned around locally to find someone to take Robert in. They all apparently asked her if we were churchgoers because if we were not, they could not have him in their houses. A strange kind of Christianity. The good doctor took Robert to her own house for the night to keep an eye on him as he really was very sick.

I stayed with the wagon and Bess and the dogs on a small patch of ground at a crossroads, with all the trees so tall above me. A police car came by and they told me to keep an eye out for a *prowler* who had been reported in the area.

I did know they were just wanting to terrify and torment me, but as it got dark and my one candle was not going to see me through until morning, I lay down in the wagon bed with the dogs, all of us under the covers. Every so often the dogs would growl and my heart would go wild, but by dawn I felt a kind of pride for having got through the night without dying – of terror.

It was quite a moment for me in that from then on, I was not so scared of everything, and not so troubled at the thought of being alone. The doctor brought Robert back, and he lay in the wagon as I harnessed up Bess and led her back onto the road.

I remember a hill, a long hill, Bess pulling an extra-heavy wagon with Robert inside it and me walking at her head leading her by her bridle. Halfway up a tourist couple jumped out from the side of the road, waving me down and asking me to stop so they could take a photograph.

'Can't stop.' I went on.

It's not all right to stop a horse in her stride on a hill and then take off again. At the top of the hill, they waited with their camera and I did stop – to rest Bess.

One of them came towards me holding out his hand and dropped a sixpence into mine. I burst into tears and he said, 'No, no, it's OK, it's nothing,' believing I was overcome with gratitude instead of just overwhelmed by the exhaustion of it all.

You're damn right it's nothing. I walked Bess on again, and refused to cry any more.

* * *

Maybe a shameful story now, but I will tell it anyway.

A few days later, with Robert better, we stopped in a lay-by to rest, light a fire and make some tea. A car drew in, and out came another couple of tourists who walked towards us saying, 'Ooh – can we buy that old thing?' They meant the wooden bellows that I used to encourage damp wood to burn. They were indeed old and the leather was split so they were not that good at blowing the flames into life.

Robert said, 'Ten pounds.'

I was speechless and about to laugh at him when they said, 'OK' and handed over ten pounds. It certainly made up for the humiliation of the sixpence but really the old thing could not have been worth anything at all.

The Revenge of the Bellows. They kept us fed for a long time.

Moorland, Late May 1969

Out of the trees and on to Rannoch Moor. Our days went walking by with no other souls – just us, the dogs, Bess and the wagon. A barren landscape of heather and moss, all sky-wide space and featureless misty horizon. Exposure.

As we stopped to rest, Robert saw a pile of rocks far across the moorland and decided he must go to visit it. I stayed with the dogs and Bess and the wagon as he set out. His figure became smaller and smaller until I thought he might just disappear – taken into the hidden fairy kingdom he had always hoped to find, never to emerge again, leaving me with my heartbeat, and the dogs and Bess and the wagon, to go back or go forward or – or what?

The road was so long, empty. But then – back in the distance – I saw a red dot. The dot became a car. A red Mini. It flashed past me in a blink, impressing upon me how slowly we had been travelling, how our footsteps and hoof beats were taking us along at just a human and horse's pace.

I stood there, seemingly invisible, but the driver must have seen that strange little green wagon with its red undercarriage and bright yellow wheels against the endless, colourless moor. And the black horse, and the young woman waving in the middle of this great bare land. But there was for me no longed-for waving back, or slowing down or ached-for link with another human being. The Mini became a small red dot again. Gone.

Fury rising. Why was I not in a car? A car with a good strong engine and a tank full of petrol, safe and insulated from the wilderness. Why were we making Bess do this? How ever did I come to be here, alone, with miles left behind me of urban and suburban roads, spring-green fields and lakes and familiar soft hills – and now miles of unknown ahead, all still to be trodden? Slow and steady pace wins the race? What was the sense in it?

Were we really saving anything of the earth's resources, as we had come to believe we were? What about the food that went into the energy we needed to get us all where we were heading, the rubber for the tyres, for our boots? The iron and steel that went into the wagon and its wheels? The iron and fire for Bess's shoes?

I remember vividly that moment of doubt – and still don't really know the answers.

* * *

Finding wood for a fire to boil the kettle was not possible on that moor. No trees. Combustible heather roots? Danger, fire, fire. Better not. No tea for Robert when he returned – without news of fairy kingdoms.

On we went.

We had been climbing slowly for days. Through Tyndrum and on, no let up for Bess, leaning hard into her collar and traces, but as we approached the jaws of Glencoe with the mountains rearing up around us, we could feel the road begin to fall away. We clambered up onto the seat of the wagon, beckoned the dogs safely inside, and black Bess started on her wild, mane-flying, glorious descent.

Free, no trudge, no doubt nor fury, just the wind in our hair, the air racing past and the joyous clatter of Bess's iron shoes as they hit the tarmac. Laughter the whole way down, a long way down, and down and round and down again. No other vehicles on the road.

As that road flattened out, a lone cottage owner allowed us to stay overnight in his field. Bess could be let out of her harness, and with no collar, no chain she was free to go peacefully grazing. In my mind I still see the kindly green of the few hardwood trees along the stone wall, the first we had sheltered under for miles and miles.

Some fallen branches. Wood for the fire.

Sweet tea at last.

Three

Laggan. At the end of Loch Lochy, where the road forks left to Laggan Locks and onward towards Fort Augustus, we found a corner where we could park the wagon. It was sun-filled there – dappling the soft young grass under the tall skinny larches, all laden with pale-green needles. I felt some kind of happiness. We had come to a good place, peace and harmony between the two of us. Water nearby, plenty of firewood, a sprung-apart rowboat on the shore, with copper rivets no longer holding it together – rivets that we prised out and put in a little bag for weighing in at the next scrapyard, if we could find one.

I sat on a bank holding Bess on a rope and halter. Her grazing of the vetches and clovers in amongst the grasses made a hypnotic, rhythmic sound. Her wide black back was warming in the sun and she seemed as sleepily content as I was. I talked to her sometimes. In that perfect moment I asked her if she thought I would ever have children and she lifted her head briefly and nodded. She nodded three times and went back to tearing lazily at the verge with her big old teeth.

Out of Our Way

The sunlit peace of that beautiful place was shattered when a taxi pulled up alongside the wagon. A young girl with a shaven head and a white dove in a cage stepped out.

She had seen our strange picture in a local Fort William newspaper, recognised Robert from having known him some time before, and so came looking for us. She was sixteen and now living with the poet Neil Oram, who had found and moved into an abandoned cottage with his wife and child, up in the hills above Loch Ness.

We were nearly at the road off to the west which would have taken us to Glenelg and the sea crossing to Kylerhea, Isle of Skye, but she persuaded us (she persuaded Robert) that we should miss our turning and keep going up the west side of Loch Ness to meet her new friends as it would be a magical place for us, so she said.

I felt the old dark dread – this would be wrong, we should keep to our own path – but I stayed quiet, invaded, my place taken.

Her dove was tame but we both tried to impress upon her that if she were to let it out of its cage our Afghan hound May would most certainly kill it.

She slept – as often our visitors did – under the wagon. The next morning as I awoke, I could hear her sobbing. I looked out and there she was in Robert's arms whilst her dove lay on the ground, feet in the air, with very red blood on its very white chest. An impassive Afghan hound stared off into the distance.

Me being me, it could not have been more of a warning to keep going on our long-planned route and not go out of our way, but out of our way we did go.

As Bess passed the road where we had intended to turn off, I felt such foreboding – as well I might.

* * *

The shortest way to Grotaig, Neil Oram's cottage, was straight up a forestry track which led off the road. Otherwise, we would have to go a few miles further up the side of the loch to Drumnadrochit and find the turning to the back road, the very long way round.

So we headed up the track with the wagon – only it was steep with loose stones and gravel; Bess slipped and went down on her knees. My heart, poor Bess, all our ignorant fault.

We took her back down to the road. I walked up the track with the dogs whilst Robert and Neil drove Bess and the wagon round the twisting, turning lochside road.

A reckless speeding car. A slow wagon. A big bang.

It must have lifted Bess off her feet, as it broke the back of the wagon and did a fair bit of damage to the car. Poor Bess again, although she did not seem very badly hurt – the broken skin on her knees the worst of it still.

The wagon was pulled up the hill by a tractor, breaking the shafts as it went around a sharp corner, then taken to the local blacksmith to be mended.

We stayed in the cottage with Neil, his wife and their young daughter. I gave them a bowl I had found on a rubbish dump the day that a small van had drawn up in a lay-by where we had been resting Bess, and the driver had wrenched open the back of the van in a fury and started to throw everything out and down the bank to join the rest of the rubbish down at the bottom.

It was clearly the contents of a house and we asked if we could have some of it, but he was in no mind to let us as he continued to angrily chuck and hurl. We rescued a few things as they tumbled down the bank: a scrubbing brush and a frying pan, some little boxes of herbs, and I caught the bowl as it rolled – a beautiful little thing with blue birds sponge-printed all around. I have been collecting similar bowls ever since.

Above Loch Ness, Midsummer

Bess hurt, wagon hurt, what next? Stuck. Staying with the poet Neil and his family – and the girl with the shaven head still grieving for her dove.

Robert went to bed. I didn't follow as I was still talking to Neil, who was listening.

My only experiences with marijuana back in London had been terrifying and the effects long lasting. Robert wanted marijuana legalised and when I had said – when we were first together – that I had had a bad time with it and that maybe it could be risky for some people, he tipped me off his knee. He said that it was just me, just my reaction because I was in some way too weak, too fearful of the very sky. Well, yes, at that time I was fearful of the very everything.

I never mentioned it again, until a year later, when talking to the poet Neil that night above Loch Ness, he described his bad time with opium. I asked if it was because he was too weak and fearful but got the answer I needed – that some people could and some could not.

We can't all, and some of us don't. That's all there is to it.
– Eeyore

I soon went to join Robert in our bed – but to his turned back. In the morning he furiously turned on me, and broke us. My wrong had been to stay up and talk to someone else whilst Robert was feeling in need of reassurance for the hard times we were having with the horse, the wagon, and all that had happened since deciding back at Laggan to stray from our original path.

* * *

I needed to see my brother. I don't remember how we got to London, I only remember waiting for a local bus down on the main road along the side of Loch Ness. Robert sitting on the grassy bank with his arms around his knees. Hunched. Eyes palest blue, almost sea-green.

As I stood and looked down at him it was as if his heart had been opened like a book and laid bare. That he had no defences and his whole life was playing out before me in sorrow and tragedy. I felt as cold as the waters of the loch.

After a few days in London to recover, me with my brother, Robert away with Robert Hewison, I hitch-hiked with John James back up to Loch Ness, back to Bess and the dogs who were being looked after by Neil and his family.

I determined that from now on I would be quite single, alone with myself, me and I, together.

* * *

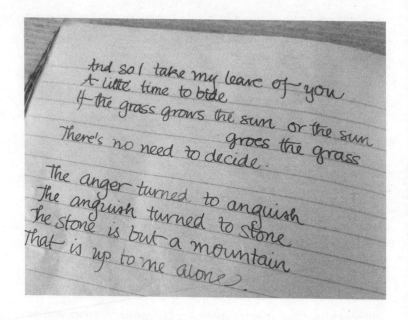

And so I take my leave of you
A little time to bide
If the grass grows the sun or the sun
grows the grass
There's no need to decide.

The anger turned to anguish
The anguish turned to stone
The stone is but a mountain
That is up to me alone.

* * *

However, Robert arrived a few days later – with Sandy, whom he had found looking confused and adrift in Trafalgar Square. She was from California and had just seen her conscripted boyfriend off to Germany where he had been stationed before possibly being sent to Vietnam. She hadn't known where to go next. Robert persuaded her to go to Scotland with him. What could she do but agree?

I guessed they were together, I would have expected that, but no, Sandy was way too good and sensible. In no little time Robert and I were back with each other, in as much as we had ever been. Why? I sigh now. I must have recovered some remnants of my compassion for him and, well, the wagon was mended and the horse recovered, a journey begun and not yet completed. So we set off with John and with Sandy, Bess, May and Blue – back, with relief, to the right way, over the hills to Skye.

Forgiveness is a longer road, but I'll get there one day.

House, August

Many more miles through the longest, loneliest glens, so different to the moors where I had felt no human life. Here there had once been people, homes, livings, families of several generations – all cleared away for sheep and profit for the landowners. People whose lives were broken, scattered to the four winds. I knew nothing of the eighteenth- and nineteenth-century Highland Clearances but when I learned about it later, I could remember the feeling of the place, the sadness of the glens, and that now all that remained of the vanished people were the stone skeletons of their houses.

Strangely there was one cottage all on its own at the side of the road, where an elderly couple came running out as we passed, maybe not having seen a soul for weeks, saying, 'Yes, hello, hello.' We stopped for a while since they were so happy to be spending a little time with us. They asked if there was anything we needed, gave us a bale of hay and some eggs and waved us sadly on our way. I'll not forget them.

I did not want to be them.

'Jog Along Bess'. A song of happy contentment, but written sitting against a stone wall in the faint mist of rain and midges, by the river in a desolate Glen Moriston. A song to keep us going – and so it did.

* * *

We arrived in the village of Glenelg after many more days of walking. We found Gavin Maxwell's empty cottage and opened the door with the key we'd been given by his friend all those miles back north of Glasgow. A roof, a bathroom, a kitchen, sheets and blankets, shelter. And a field for Bess.

Looking at the rain map for Scotland, Glenelg is about the wettest place on it – and it did rain the whole time we were there. Sandy from California could not imagine why anyone would want to live in Scotland – her experience was surely of damp and grey, and being a southerner myself it seemed all wrong that August was not filled with sunny days. Sandy had never in her life been without the sun on her body and she hated being so pale. I had not lived in Scotland long enough by then, but by now I would be able to tell her that there is more to it than year-round sunshine.

Robert's wisdom tooth blew up. The local doctor said he had to go over to Skye to the nearest dentist. It was not in our plans that his first steps onto Skye would be this way, but he was taken over and his tooth was wrenched out, he was brought back and put to bed.

Our May got out one moonlit night and found a flock of sheep to chase – right off a cliff. Off a *cliff*. Both Robert and I were so horrified with her that we would have let her be shot had it become known that it had been our dog, but John was just horrified with *us*, that we would ever think to allow her death. So he took her and left to go back to London – where she caught a white poodle in a park. He still adored her, and she him, and she lived the rest of her life with him. They were so alike that when she sat next to him from behind you could not tell whose black shaggy hair was whose.

I missed them both. Sandy went away, back to California, and I missed her too.

Robert took a while to recover from the big hole in his jaw, but maybe it was good to be just us again and enjoy the best of us, and rekindle our reasons for being there. We watched the seals, and the killer whales as they came through the narrow strip of sea between Glenelg and Kylerhea over on Skye. Every day we walked on the rocky and seaweedy beach in the rain and I pined a bit for the summer seasides of southern England, but slowly settled into the way of the north-western skies. I was – after all – looking for the wild.

Before we could take the little car ferry to Kylerhea we had to wait until a promised inspection from an insurance man for the driver of the speeding car that had crashed into the back of the wagon on the shore of Loch Ness, lifting Bess off her feet. The wagon had been well repaired but even so, when he eventually turned up, that man was very pleased to tell us that our dandelion wheels had undoubtedly once belonged to a 1908 Morris Cowley – and he astonishingly awarded us £150. Not there and then, we would have to wait for it, but knowing it would come to us some time was immense – a huge sum for us.

It was of course Bess who had suffered the damage. Her spine must have been injured, as she developed a strange limping gait in her later years.

———

Nearly There

It had been over a year but here we were on Skye. The crossing had been short and so sweet, on a small ferry with room for just a few cars, and our one horse-drawn vehicle. There was no bridge yet. The other, bigger ferry from Kyle of Lochalsh was the usual crossing with better, maybe flatter roads each side, but I remember with gratitude our gift of the key and the directions to the house in Glenelg as a bit of an oasis, even in the rain.

We were nearing Donovan and our friends in Stein, at

the top end of Skye, but by now we were not in much of a hurry. More miles did not trouble us and even the dark spiky harshness of the Cuillin Hills did not worry me too much. Mountains hadn't hurt me so far and so I was no longer in as much fear of them.

The midges on Skye were unlike anything I had known on the mainland. Their bites were nasty, and there were so many, in great black clouds. We helped some crofters dig peat, out on a bog, and they seemed almost immune to the little creatures. We were advised not to swat at them. 'Kill one and a *thousand* will come to the funeral,' we were told. They did.

We stopped one Saturday evening on a patch of grass by a small white church. By Sunday we were told to move, and when we protested, saying our horse needed to rest and that we were not doing any harm, we were told – darkly, from the church door – 'animals are low in the dust'. We moved on, far away, away from the church.

We met an American in Portree harbour, living on a boat with a young girl. I remember (whether rightly or not) that he had been a nuclear physicist and had impressively given it all up. Robert got on very well with him, and was introduced to the I Ching, the Book of Changes. This was important – to Robert – for all of the years we were together (or not), as a guide, and a consolation in hard times. It scared the wits out of me as any kind of divination always did. However, whenever I did get something right, I would mutter 'perseverance furthers' to myself. I still do.

* * *

I really don't know what I expected to find when reaching
Donovan, his islands and our old friends. We had not been
in contact at all since we'd left Seagull's Rest and by now
Robert and I were very different people, for sure, to the ones
who had set off all that time ago. We had become self-
sufficient in a way I had not expected, but it felt good. One
of the joys of the journey had been the times I ran ahead and
watched Robert and that little green wagon, coming towards
me with everything that we could possibly need to be going
on with. Our Bessie and my Blue. The battered old bucket
swinging on a hook underneath, the patchwork curtains
made out of materials that had history from even way back
in my childhood, the bow saw, the pans and the kettle, my
guitar, and the paintings on the inside walls that John and
Sam had sent us off with, dreamscapes of all our futures.

Bess and wagon

The turning to Stein was at the Fairy Bridge. Nearly there. We were resting at the side of the road when a Land Rover swept by, braked hard and reversed. It was Donovan, and Sam the painter. Nobody knew we were coming, they all probably thought that we'd have given up just north of London, but they had recently heard we were on Skye and had tracked us – they said – by the blackened turf from the fires we had left along the way.

Donovan sat up on the wagon and we walked a few yards with him, but since we were still at least a day's travel to go, we left Bess tied up, climbed into the Land Rover and were driven the rest of the way.

This arrival should have felt like the end of the rainbow, after all the sun and rain and windy miles we had trodden to get there. But it didn't take long to realise there was no place for us, nowhere for Bess, nowhere for the wagon. Two seasons' worth of vegetable gardens had been dug, some of the diggers had gone back to London, any available cottages were all taken, even the ruins, and the Schoolhouse kept for Donovan whenever he was back from world-touring and stadium-filling. I learned that he was not often there, so it was pure chance that we arrived when he was visiting. Much had happened to him since I'd last seen him – as well as to us. All of us so different now.

I borrowed his guitar and sang 'Rainbow River'. There were flickers of recognition across his face and in his eyes. The way I sang 'disturb the ground' with the emphasis on 'dis' was very much him. The last music I had listened to was his own back at Seagull's Rest – I'd had no record player nor radio since – only me and my guitar – and so his way with words would have been in my head, I'm sure.

Nothing was said.

Bess never made it to Donovan's land – we were taken back to her in the Land Rover. I don't remember being in any way upset or saddened by this sudden change to our inner landscape. I could be in the *now* rather than 'Travelling Towards a Hebridean Sun'. I liked it.

The decision was made to leave Skye behind and go even further west – over the sea to the outer islands – to look for Mac and Iris and then to seek a place for ourselves.

Turn Around, Keep Going

Bess and the wagon were turned around and we made for the car ferry from the port of Uig to Lochmaddy, on North Uist, Outer Hebrides.

We arrived in Lochmaddy in the middle of a dark night. Bess had been so terrified during the crossing – tied up and skidding with her iron shoes on the lurching, wet steel deck – that we had not been able to leave her, either of us, for a minute. If one of us started to go she let out a whinny of such distress we could not move. She had never before expressed any need of us whatsoever, as if we were not born Travellers, only playing at it and that she was just along for the ride. Some ride.

We came off the boat into pitch blackness, found the nearest piece of ground which felt like grass, gave Bess some oats and got ourselves into the wagon bed for the night. In the morning we looked out to find a bleak, treeless and barren landscape which only now, more than fifty years down the line, can I begin to think of as beautiful.

Lochmaddy was as deserted and friendless a place as it is possible to imagine. At first light it was only grey, with a few straggling houses and leaning telegraph poles, smiling like a mouth with missing teeth. A flat road wandered off into the further greyness.

It was a shock. Skye had been beautiful – but the Outer Hebridean islands can take some getting used to. Then they bind some with their magic; a magic I found to be too strange to enchant me – yet.

We found our 'Window Over the Bay' by chance a week or so later. We were told about the Isle of Berneray, a small island off the north of Uist, and how pretty it was, and so we left Bess in the care of Mac and Iris Macfarlane – who we had found in their, by now, newly roofed croft house – and took the small ferry one morning. There was just one road on the island and we walked to the end of it, the south end. The clouds opened and we ran into the doorway of a ruined thatched longhouse for shelter.

That was the house we ended up with, moving in to the one end with a bit of turf roof still intact. We typically misheard the name of it as 'Fairy Cottage'. That was enough for us. In fact, it was the old Ferry Cottage where once the boats had come in from Uist. Now they came in to a small harbour further up the island where the shop and post office and a few two-storey 'white' houses were scattered up the hill from the jetty. There was no causeway, not even planned as yet – that came after we were long gone.

The horse, well, there was no boat big enough to take her to the island; all the cows and sheep had either been made to swim over behind a rowboat or had been born there. It turned out that each crofter was allowed two cows or one horse on the common grazing. There were no horses left on the island. Swimming our horse over would go against the islanders' grain, not that *not* having her there would have meant they could have had two more cows, but that was not the point.

There were people living on Berneray who had moved over from Uist a few miles away in 1940 but were still regarded with suspicion. No one could believe that we were there out of choice. Who would be? We were thought by some to be spies as we spent a lot of time gazing out to sea at the sunset – in the direction of the American base on the island of Benbecula. Reluctantly, we had to leave Bess with Mac and Iris on Uist for the time being.

We bought our house for £150, the insurance settlement from the time a speeding car ploughed into the back of the wagon on the shores of Loch Ness. The cheque was cashed for us by Mac and Iris, but after a week or two on Berneray we realised that probably all we had bought of Ferry Cottage was what was left of the turf roof. Crofting law can have the hardiest lawyer in tears, and we knew nothing of it. The family who had sold us the house – and a piece of land about it – could only speak Gaelic, and we could not.

The Justice of the Peace lived in a dark, forbidding house at the other end of the island and he had been brought out for the signing of the receipt. He must have known but didn't seem to care that the family were selling us something that was not theirs to sell.

Not that we really minded when we found out. We genuinely planned to be there for life, and had faith we would sort out the ownership as time went by. It was late September and we had by then come to like the island. The white sand beaches down the west coast, the clear turquoise sea and the many wild flowers in the 'machair' – as the grasslands were called on the Atlantic side of the island. One of our windows was over the cockle bay behind the house.

A door between the part we lived in and the even more derelict part had a doorknob fashioned out of a bunch of rusty nails. Like a small bouquet, it made me realise that the people who had lived there would have had to make do in ways that I could never have imagined. No hardware shops, mail orders would arrive after months maybe, and so the best was made of what was to hand.

There was a standpipe and tap in a pile of rocks just outside the door and even though the constant wind blew the water out horizontally so my bucket had to be tipped sideways to catch it – making me laugh – just the fact that we had arrived there settled me down for a while.

Afraid that anyone on the island might find out that we were not married, I started to call myself Vashti Lewis, and Robert found a copper plumber's washer that I put onto my wedding finger. I used the ashes from the fire to polish it up, bright and golden, but sometimes I forgot and my finger would go green around it as the shine faded. Maybe suspicions were raised as we were asked if we had any wedding photos. I found the one that Anthony McCall had taken of us in the back of a car on our way to a concert – just before we'd set off with Bess. I had a piece of lace in my hair, and a white Victorian petticoat as a dress. That would do, and it did.

In the back of Happiness Runs

A young boy called Alan who lived with his four siblings, mother and grandmother in a small thatched cottage along the shore, shyly befriended us and told us how he longed to escape the island. He had tried building a raft but that hadn't worked out. His father was a seafaring man, and this is what Alan wanted to be too. Robert had written 'Trawlerman's Song' to my tune, and I taught it to Alan on my recorder. He borrowed the recorder and came back the next day – playing the song perfectly.

My favourite memory of that wild and clever wee boy is from when I was walking back with him to his grandmother's house, heads down against a gale. As I realised we were no longer side by side I looked back and there he was – in a ditch – where he had been blown right off his little feet. He was unhurt and we laughed into the wind all the rest of the way.

On Uist there were new houses built next to the old abandoned thatched cottages, and just before Robert and I moved to Berneray we had found a pine dresser and a box bed in one of the ruins, and an ancient, rusty, free-standing cast-iron stove called a 'Modern Mistress' in another. We'd asked if we could have them and they were kindly sent over to Berneray for us on the ferry boat, the furniture broken down and 'flat-packed'. It all sat on the dockside for a while as we had no way to transport it to our house. My lovely brother came up from London for a short visit and it was a wonder to us what his five-pound note could achieve. The stove was delivered on the forks of a tractor, hoving over the hill with its cabriole legs in the air, the furniture bouncing on the trailer behind.

The stove was installed in the old fireplace, and having an oven and hotplates after so long cooking on an open fire was a great joy. We rebuilt the box bed and it sheltered us from the wind that blew through the holes in our walls. The still-flat pine dresser became much-needed kindling when a guest did not recognise it as a piece of antique Hebridean furniture and set about it with an axe – long since forgiven.

Sound Techniques

Our neighbour Wally Dix – more of whom later – had a telephone. She kindly took calls for us and one came in October from Joe Boyd. He wanted to keep his promise to record an album with me at the end of our horse-drawn journey, and was checking to see if I had written enough songs yet. If so, he would book a studio in London. I don't remember how I felt about going away again, but if Joe had kept his word then I was going to have to keep mine.

Joe sent Christopher Sykes to collect us for the drive down in his old Morris Minor which he called The Kettle since it regularly boiled over, causing him to have to stop every few miles to top up the radiator.

Christopher accidentally backed over my guitar as we were packing to leave, cracking its neck completely and making it unplayable, but he had a friend – Alice Ormsby-Gore – who he said had been given a similar guitar by Eric Clapton, about the same size and shape but it had mother-of-pearl flowers inlaid all over it, not just around the sound hole. After we'd arrived in London he asked her to lend it to me for the sessions and she kindly agreed. It felt so unlike mine, it looked perfect, shiny, unplayed, unbefriended ever in its life. To me it sounded like blotting paper rather than the deep and familiar sounds I grieved for in my own, time-worn one, but I got used to its strange ways after a few days.

By the time I came to record the album, I'd written songs like 'Jog Along Bess', which Joe wasn't so keen on. He had liked the more romantic ones, but I had become so immersed in the life and the journey and the animals and all of it, that I was documenting them too. I think his heart sank, but he didn't say so – not to me.

Whilst in London I discovered that I was pregnant. I was so very happy, but it didn't delight my family much, and Robert wasn't over the moon. It wasn't in his plans – he was only twenty-three and I was twenty-four. Some of what I hear now in the recording of the songs is my quiet joy, as well as apprehension. And as soon as I knew I was pregnant I didn't write another song. It wasn't that I didn't try to write more, because I did – but nothing happened. I wondered, well, I have wanted this child for so long, and didn't know if I would ever be able to have children, and so maybe that desire had been the songs. It felt as if all of that need and yearning had gone into the music, and once I had my child the songs never came again. And they really, truly, didn't until my last one left home, thirty-three years later. I'm not proud of that. I should have been able to do both.

The songs were recorded in Sound Techniques, off the Kings Road, over three separate evenings. Everything that was recorded was released – there were no outtakes. I did have a couple of other songs, but I thought they were too fey even for me to attempt.

Joe invited the other musicians. I'd met Robin Williamson of the Incredible String Band, but had no idea who Simon Nicol and Dave Swarbrick of Fairport Convention were. (I'd only heard of Fairport Convention because somebody had once handed me a piece of paper with their name and a phone number on it, saying this band was looking for a female singer. I ignored it, still being determined to make it on my own.) I'd been so used to singing and playing guitar by myself that it was a shock to be with others – it felt unreal.

I was to rehearse with Robin the night before the first session, at Christopher's house, and that was my first brush with Scientology. I was cooking supper in the kitchen, I came through to the sitting room, and Robin's girlfriend Janet had Robert wired up to an E-meter. *What's this?* I was instinctively wary. I was always a loner and had never, ever felt the need to align myself with anything, whereas Robert was more open to the new. He wondered and learned enthusiastically about everything, and took on different ideas, changing like a chameleon to match the day and the people within it. I could see this happening, and so I dismantled him from the wires. He didn't often take any notice of me, what I said, but he did about that. I've no idea why. Maybe he felt it too.

The first recording night was with Robin, John James and Christopher Sykes, and we just improvised. Christopher's piano playing and John on dulcitone were both so perfect for the songs and they understood completely. Robin was wonderful with 'Rose Hip November' (my favourite of all, by the way), and realised its mood and seemed to throw himself into it, but his fiddle on 'Jog Along Bess' wasn't what I had in mind at all – though I didn't, couldn't, say so at the time. (When I listen to it now I pan it to one side where it is just me and Christopher – and that is how it should have been. Robin was kind to be playing on it at all – but it just wasn't the way I imagined the song.)

The second night was when Robert Kirby, who'd been working with Joe on Nick Drake's music, brought in his beautiful arrangements, and classical musicians for the string and recorder parts. Hearing them was extraordinary for me, because the way that he'd written for the string quartet and the five recorders was so near to what was in my mind for the album, which was more of a classical feel than a folk one.

For all these years I've felt guilty about the way I behaved with Robert Kirby. He'd arranged 'Rainbow River', but had made some key changes to the third verse that I didn't like. And so the young woman who knows nothing about music – and who usually says not a word to anyone – says, 'I don't like that, can you repeat what you've done in the second verse for the third?' And so that's what he did.

He had also written a lovely part for solo violin on 'Swallow Song', but I said to the violinist with his Stradivarius, 'Do you think you could do it without vibrato?' I don't think he'd played without vibrato since he was three. He was understandably horrified but he did it. I thought it was slightly out of tune, maybe because he didn't know how to play in the plain way that I had in my head – or the way I might have played it myself had I been able to.

The third evening Joe brought Dave Swarbrick and Simon Nicol to the studio. I was amazed at how easily they took up the tunes, and we recorded three songs in three takes. I was very uncertain when they started playing mandolin and banjo on 'Come Wind Come Rain' – I liked it, but it was a bit folksy, and Joe had us all standing around one microphone to record it. I'm often called a folk singer now, largely because of the String Band and Fairport musicians Joe asked to accompany me on the recordings. They were always the well-known ones and I was the unknown, so for a long time the album was mostly only of any interest to their followers.

(Many, many years later Joe turned to me during a Q&A session after a showing of Kieran Evans's film about the 'Diamond Day' journey, *From Here to Before*, and said he had to apologise to me for bringing in members of Fairport Convention and the Incredible String Band to accompany me and so forever condemning me to being called a folk singer, something I have always complained about. It isn't as if I know *what* to call myself, but I am not and never was a folk singer. His excuse was – he said – that he had come to visit us in a field in the Lake District and I had been living the most folkie life of anyone he knew, what with the horse and the wagon, dogs and all. Well, it wasn't a field, we were in a house, but I accepted his apology.)

I didn't have any great musical ambition any more and so didn't speak up for myself enough. Recording was something I was doing because the opportunity was there, because Joe Boyd had kept his promise. But I'd just found out I was pregnant, I was about to go back to the Outer Hebrides and make my life up there, still needing to get Bess over to the island and so had other considerations at that time. After the sessions I more or less forgot about the recording for a while.

Back Home

On our return to the Hebrides just before Christmas, we found to our amazement and shock that Bess had given birth to a filly foal. She had been in a field with a small brown and white stallion some of the previous winter in the Lake District. However, since mares only usually conceive in summertime, and after our attempt at pairing her up with a beautiful thoroughbred had failed, we had assumed she was too old. The terrible regret we felt at having worked her up long hard hills pulling our house and belongings was heightened when the foal, black and white and sturdy-looking, developed pneumonia. The vet knew not what to do, nor did he seem to worry or care much, and that beautiful foal died next morning in the stable on Uist where Bess was being so kindly looked after by Mac and Iris.

Heavily in heart, we went back to Berneray. There we found our house completely green on the inside. Every surface was mouldy. With no fire and no heat and all closed up for six weeks the damp had been able to creep in. Our neighbour gave us shelter for the first week as we cleaned and dried it all out. During the tidying I realised that someone had been into the house, gone through our belongings and taken the receipt for the house. Somebody must have been very worried about the sale.

Letters to the factor – the land agent for the actual owners of the house – went unacknowledged and gradually we began to realise just how unwelcome we were amongst the younger islanders who seemed to hold the power. We had a lot of generous help from some extraordinary people, but those who were anxious to get rid of us were doing a good job.

Our greatest weakness was the horse. There seemed little point in our being there if Bess could not be with us. We went to every house to ask for help to bring her to the island. Each one in turn said it was all right by them, that it was someone else who was objecting. We could find not a soul to lend us a boat to swim her over.

Then I started to hear stories about the elderly doctor on Uist who was looking after my pregnancy. The worst was that of a young boy on an outlying island who had needed a measles vaccine. It was to be given in three doses but the doctor was not too happy about making three trips and so gave it all in one. It was said that the boy died. Whether old gossip or not, the tale so scared me that I began to secretly long for the imagined safety of the south.

* * *

Mac and Iris needed to return to England for a week and so asked us to come over from Berneray to look after Bess at their house on Uist. The house and their vegetable garden where the previous summer I had apologised to the broccoli as I cut it – my thinking being that this was the plant's potential flowering and in picking it I was depriving it of progeny, something dear to my heart. Still seems reasonable to me.

When Mac and Iris came back we felt that it was time for us to take Bess and find her somewhere else to be. The wagon too.

Where

North Uist is a large and sparsely populated island. It was January and I was three months pregnant, but not wanting to outstay our welcome we harnessed Bess up in the morning and set off down Locheport and onto the road to the north of the island. All our possessions were across the sea on Berneray, the wagon was empty, we had no blankets and little food. We walked. The Hebridean winter brings sundown early and as it started to get dark, we still had no idea where we were going.

A Land Rover passed us and drew up ahead of us. A man and a woman came back and asked us *what* we were doing.

'Looking for somewhere to keep our horse and this wagon.'

'Oh well you'd better come to us then, we're just up the road.'

They drove off, it started to snow and the dark came down. Up the road turned out to be many miles. Our hands went past that stage of coldness where they swell and feel quite warm again, but Bess was shivering. We followed our directions and found a long track turning off the road, walked head down until at last we were passing through a stone arch into a circular courtyard.

There was a large oak door up some steps at the other side of the courtyard and so we knocked. As it opened our

Land Rover man stood looking at us – with a whisky glass in his hand.

'Hello? Oh it's *you*, do come in and have a drink.'

'What about our horse?'

'Ah.'

We were shown to a stable and given straw to rub Bess down, oats and water for her, and an invitation to the house. They didn't seem to mind our wild hair and shiny, snow-blown faces, our wet clothes, or the dripping dog.

They were Fergus and Doon Granville, lairds, owners of the Isle of North Uist. We sat down to dinner in their circular house, at one end of a long, polished mahogany table with candles in silver candelabra, crystal wine glasses and fine porcelain plates. Robert told our ragged story.

Later, shown to a bedroom with curved wall, white carpet, big window to the dark sea and a great big feather bed – a knock on the door brought someone from the kitchen with a little bowl of nicely cut-up raw steak for Blue. He had no idea what to do with it having lived on mostly brown bread, porridge and eggs like us. Ah my Blue, whoever could understand a dog turning his nose up like that? I had to say I was very sorry, 'But could he have some scrambled eggs, please?'

Returning to our bedroom after the next morning's break-fast, we found our bed made and our wet outdoor clothes from the day before dried and folded neatly on the chairs.

A picnic lunch was made up for us in the kitchen and we were directed to a part of the shore where Fergus Granville was quite sure he had found fairy footprints. I think that maybe when he realised we did not raise any eyebrows about his conviction that fairy people, the Little People, had once lived on his land he was happy to educate us more about what he knew of them. Robert believed completely and understood. Which was just as well.

We parked the wagon in a field near the shore and set Bess free – free as she would stay for more than a year – and we were driven to the ferry to go back to our derelict old house on Berneray.

A week later Doon sent a crate of oranges over to the island for me.

———

Voices

Someone said – when I related this story to him – 'Well maybe it was because of your classy accent that you got entry in to all these places?'

Me?

All right, I had been sent to private schools – privileged against my will since I had pleaded to be able to go to the same school as my local friends, but it had never crossed my mind how Robert and I would be perceived. Although maybe it should have – from our experiences with the police.

They regularly approached us because we had been reported to them by people who did not want us in their villages, or wanted us moved on from where we had drawn onto a verge or a patch of rough ground, and then their attitude changed as they realised we were not Romany, nor tinkers, those whom they habitually abused and mostly still do.

I think about the Traveller woman who taught me about drying the washing on the thorn bushes and keeping everything in bags, who had taken a look at me then looked at Robert then back at me and said, 'Well you're one of us but he ain't.' How I swelled with pride, for my distant relations who were now maybe closer than I had ever dared believe. And, it was something I was that Robert wasn't. Why did that please me so? I must have felt very much the lesser being in our lives together for it to have meant so much to me.

I'm still not really sure what I am, but the fact that I might be judged by what I sounded like had never occurred to me. And anyway, I never spoke a word to anyone if I could help it.

Would the Granvilles on North Uist have rescued us if we had not had 'educated' voices? Would Mac and Iris have trusted us with their Lakeland house for a whole winter? I'll never know.

But what did the Traveller family on the rubbish tip in Derby who brought us fish and chips care, or the scrappie in Lancaster who allowed me to take whatever I wanted from his day's collecting, or the Cumbrian hill farmer's wife who, without even asking us what we wanted, laughed as she saved us from the weather? Or the kind Golden Virginia and Golden Wonder farmer, and so many others who had been good to us along the way?

It may be that since we had little money, no homes to return to, and no apparent feeling for riches that we were quite set apart from the usual perceptions of class or status. We were different, on a journey with a destination in mind, eccentric and – yes – a little crazy, but maybe that's what some people liked about us. We certainly seemed to mystify the police which was in itself a bit of a joy.

Skies

Midwinter Berneray. The sky so big – sometimes different in every corner, blue, cloudy, sunny, wild. The winds could blow us backwards, and the long white beach on the west would throw up driftwood which we collected for the stove. There was no peat on the island, only the coal which came over in a small boat from Harris.

Robert and I had intended to make our lives there on Berneray but by early spring the hostility from some of the islanders began to make itself felt. Whilst walking the mile from the island shop with a sack of coal on my back and six months pregnant I was passed not only by the waving postman in his van but by the shopkeeper and the young ferrymen in theirs. One ferryman had told friends from the south who planned to surprise us with a visit that we were not there, and so they went away. Backs were turned as I went in through the shop doorway, and voices that had been speaking in English turned to Gaelic. I can't hear the Gaelic even now without remembering.

There is no blame. We were two idiot dreamers who chose the wrong island to carry out those dreams upon. We had no business there. Our attitude was patronising, assuming old was best and that we could relive the past there, but the recent history of the island was of relentless struggle with poverty, climate, oppressive landlords and a feeling that the rest of the world thought them primitive.

Berneray held its ancient history near to the surface. With no trees, the only verticals being the new electricity poles, Viking days hung in the air with nothing to absorb them. Gales flew around our frail old roof, made the beams move above us, and bits of turf and blackened cobwebs drop into our porridge. Our neighbour filled us with ghostly tales whilst we sat at her feet and dared not go home for fear of the spectres who would accompany us to our door until we could find matches for the lamp. The sun rose at ten and was gone by three. The stove which I blacked with Zebrite in turn blacked me, and the wind browned our faces and hands as we set about mending our old Ferry Cottage.

Arriving as we did with almost nothing – me in my long brown tweed dress and wellington boots, Robert in his beard and patched trousers – must have brought back to the older islanders too many images of hardship and heartbreak. We loved the old thatched 'black' houses; they were upset by them. We liked the oil lamps; they were throwing them out onto the rocks as the electricity poles arrived. We enjoyed the fiddle music, which died with the first TV. We listened to dark songs sung by a woman in a deep and ancient voice whilst the rest of the island shunned her.

As hard as we were trying to turn back the hands of time, Berneray was aching to drive them forward. There were days where I found what I was looking for – such as the harvesting, the scything of the barley, the stooking of the straw with grain still attached, the skilful building of the round stacks next to the croft houses, the potato howking with a big iron hook, on my knees in the earth with a woman who kept one sack for herself, sent one to her daughter in Glasgow and gave me the other one for the help. There was the widow who gave us a good meal every Sunday night if we would only go to the church.

We went to the church; we would certainly have been driven off the island if we had not. I am haunted by memory of the beautiful call-and-response music that sounded like centuries of the Atlantic wailing through the church roof-beams, but I forget the extra sermons (in English especially for us) which preached against the evils of the mainland. 'The lord walks in the Islands' and avoids the dark satanic mills – of Inverness.

The people I remember with grateful fondness in fact were all women. Mrs Mackinnon, who was long widowed, and Miss Macleod were a year later to send a hessian sack with a tied-on label addressed to 'Robert and Vashti Lewis, Galway, Ireland', and it reached us. Inside were twelve pairs of knitted socks (the older women knitted socks with off-cuts of wool from the tweed weavers, then traded them at the shop for groceries) and a huge brown wool coat for Robert which had belonged to Mrs Mackinnon's husband.

The most memorable was our aforementioned neighbour, Mrs Kate Dix. She had spent twenty years of her married life in Sunderland and was at eighty-three wise, brittle and good, truly good, not good because she should be. Nicknamed Wally (the Walrus) for her habit when younger of swimming in the sea every day of the year, her house (Tigh Wally) was a round Nissen hut with tongue-and-groove lining, wall-papered over in 1930s bungalow style. She always had a fine fire going in her pink-tiled fireplace and a barley broth on to simmer. She gave us milk every day, and if we didn't collect it on time, she poured it into the wheelbarrow at her door which she had just used for cleaning out the byre. Her one cow was her pride, her yearly calves regularly winning prizes for their hefty weight.

Her morning greeting to Robert was always 'Come in y'old cac' (shit) as she wrenched open the door before we could knock, and with hands clasped behind her bent back, stamped back down her corridor. This was her inviting us in for a cup of tea. We knew she knew we were coming over because we had seen her binoculars blinking in the sunlight through her window.

She viewed me with despair, thinking me more than a little daft and in need of some looking after, but she had never shown affection in her life for any but her immediate family. When her calf was ill that winter, she took to her bed for a week and her daughter had to come over from Harris to take care of her and the calf. We were all concerned for her, but it became apparent that she was grieving for the calf and that her religion forbade her from feeling for the beast. She feared punishment for her grief in the form of something bad happening to one of her own.

She recovered well enough, as did the calf, for the next visit by the man from the School of Scottish Studies in Edinburgh. He came out every six months or so to collect stories from Wally Dix, the Bardess. She told us that she would often listen to the morning story on the BBC, translate it into Gaelic and with a few little twists speak it into his tape recorder. Whether true or not she clearly delighted in getting one over on the academics.

She apparently lived well into her nineties, every evening head down against the wind to the shore, waving her stick and both arms, and shouting for her 'Gealachas' to come in from the machair for milking. The first time I had seen her do this I thought she was shouting at me. It was just her way. And mine.

* * *

The April day we finally left Berneray I was at last given a lift by tractor to the boat. Scruff the old ferryman placed his large rheumaticky hand on my backside and hoisted me onto the trailer. I turned round to say goodbye and his very blue eyes twinkled at me out of his terrible old face and he said 'We'll see you again.'

Scruff

No, you will not, I thought. We tried our very best to make our lives here, but without any hope of bringing our Bess over to be with us there was little point in our staying. I was also becoming more and more afraid as I did not want to take any more risks with this baby of mine.

Resisting the urge to punch Scruff for everything that had gone before – for the collective effort to make life as difficult for us as some of them could – I did feel a pang for leaving the illusion we had journeyed so long and so hard towards. For leaving the possibilities we had planted the seeds for, for knowing that I could have persevered for twenty years and possibly achieved some kind of acceptance. Regret also for leaving those dignified elderly women of Berneray who had given me much in the short time I had known them. Not just socks for my feet and broth for my growing belly, but thoughts for my head which would stay with me always.

Theirs was a life of quiet acceptance, and keen rebellion in undercover ways.

Like helping the *hippies* at Ferry.

Trees and Green and Guitar,
Spring 1970

We had walked, argued, fought, loved, laughed, cried, ridden and ferried from south of London to the Outer Hebrides over two summers and two winters, with a few trips back south and north again, mostly in John James's car Happiness Runs and Christopher Sykes's The Kettle. But now I flew back from Benbecula – the island between South and North Uist – to London, via Glasgow, in a few hours. Robert had Blue and so took a bit longer by ferry, bus and train.

We left Bess and the wagon where they were for the time being, safe with the Granvilles on North Uist.

Journey's End

Moving into a shed-house in my brother's garden in Sussex, it was strange to be suddenly amongst gently swaying trees, daffodils, bright-green mown grass. I missed the sky, and the distances. I missed the clear turquoise sea and long, empty, white-sand beaches. I missed our independence, but I felt safer not to be planning to have my baby on a small island, in a still-falling-down black house with an earth floor, under cobwebby sooty rafters in a raging gale. It was also good to be near my sister-in-law, Inda, who had become my surrogate mother in many ways. She is only four and a half years older than me but says she still thinks of me as one of her children. I wonder why.

My main memory of this time waiting for the baby is the story of that 'old banjo thing' my aunt had given me back in Leek – the guitar that Christopher Sykes accidentally ran over when we were leaving Berneray to go to London for the recording. Probably from the mid-nineteenth century, it was apparently one of a pair that my grandfather had bought, many years before it came to me, when he was an amateur antique dealer.

Grandpa Bunyan was a tall, elegant man with snow-white hair and a large, impeccably neat moustache turned up at the ends. He carried a cane with which he would imperiously stop the traffic anywhere he wanted to cross the road. It always stopped.

D'Arcy Albert Bunyan

I don't think he ever said a word to me, not that anybody really did, now I come to think about it, but sometimes on his rare visits to London he would walk me home from school through the narrow and mostly derelict streets between Gloucester Place and Baker Street where we would visit several junk shops, dusty-windowed and dark. One, I remember clearly, had violins strung on a wire across its window. Grandpa's purchases were nearly always damaged in some way – as if he were rescuing beautiful things that might otherwise be overlooked.

The pair to my guitar had apparently been black, also inlaid with flowers – and was said to have been used as a cricket bat by my brother and sister before I was born, and so did not survive, but the other one was put away in an attic, a little cracked, some of the ivory binding missing. By the time it was given to me by my aunt years later the neck was coming apart and had to be kept together by a capo, but it had a lovely sound and many songs were written with its help.

Maybe it was the capo being fixed five frets up the neck, but with it still tuned to E A D G B E, that it had a softer more mellow sound than it might otherwise have had.

Joe Boyd knew of a lute maker who said he would be able to mend the guitar after its road accident, and so I had given it up to him whilst in London for the recording of *Just Another Diamond Day*.

I was about eight months pregnant when I got the call that it was ready to be collected. The night before we were to go up to London for it I shook Robert awake, hysterical because I'd dreamt the lute maker had taken off the machine heads and replaced them with ugly new ones. The clearest of nightmares.

Who knows, maybe it means that a musical instrument can become so much a part of a person that it even makes its way into dreams?

The lute maker wasn't in when I went to collect the guitar, but his wife brought it to me clearly expecting me to be delighted. I screamed and made her jump. The machine heads *had* been replaced, by what looked as if they belonged on a modern country and western guitar, bright white and chrome where the originals had been old brass and faded ivory. All the white binding around the edge of the body had been removed and filled in with thick black paint. Two little squares of mother-of-pearl had been inlaid each side of the bridge for no reason I could ever imagine.

Yes, the neck was repaired and it was now playable, but it sounded oh so different, harsh, all its familiar mellowness gone.

Robert, ignoring protests, went into the lute maker's workshop and found my original machine heads on a hook and so he took them back. One of the ivory posts was cracked but could have been easily mended. Such big holes had been bored into the guitar's head to accommodate the posts of the new tuners that it would be very difficult now to put the old ones back.

I never did play it again. It stayed with me – in wagons and on walls. The old machine heads were kept through the years – until my sixteen-year-old son Leif one day brought the guitar down off the wall, blew off the dust and took it into our workshop. He found some bone to repair the cracked winding post, he carefully inlaid the holes in the head with wooden bushes so that the old posts would again fit, and gave me back my beloved guitar. I taught him to play it.

I gave it to Leif when he went to live in California a few years later. The neck was broken again on the flight.

He mended it, made a good job of it, but it now hangs on his wall with old strings and desert dust.

One day I hope we might find someone who will be able to replace the white binding and bring this small guitar back to the beauty that should never have been taken from it. Maybe Leif's son Riley will play it.

It Was Different Then

Queen Charlotte's Hospital, London, July 16th 1970.

I lay in a hospital bed, in the labour ward of a big teaching hospital in London, and I was yelling, 'If anyone had told me it would be like this, I would never have fucking done it. Fuck, FUCK.'

A midwife peeled my clenched fingers one by one from the cast-iron bed bars above my head, saying sternly, 'Be quiet Mrs Bunyan or you will upset the other mothers.' I had already objected to being called Mrs when I was not Mrs anyone, but had been told I had to be addressed as Mrs – or it might again upset the other mothers. Other mothers were indeed superior beings to me as I was unmarried.

Robert, the baby's father, was not allowed to be with me for the birth – as we were unmarried. Not that he planned to be there, he didn't want to be with me at all but he was. He didn't want to come with me in the ambulance, but he did. He didn't want to stay for the birth, but he stayed. He was let in after the baby was born, dressed in a green gown with his hair sticking out from under a green bonnet, and his eyes sparkling over his mask. He was at last happy.

However, within a few moments of our son Leif being born the midwife asked if I would be having the baby adopted.

This brought to my horrified mind a very young woman I had known in 1965. She told me she had once been in a mother and baby home where she had nursed her child for six long weeks before he was taken from her and adopted by a stranger. Her parents had disowned her, the father was also young and unable to support them, so she was made to feel that she had no option but to give her baby away. There was no help to be had, it was the price to be paid for the wickedness of having a child out of wedlock. Her story, her unimaginable grief and that of so many like her, stayed with me.

As I awoke after the birth of my second child Whyn Beshlie in 1973, I foggily realised I was being asked if I would have the baby adopted, and was also being told that they could offer me a sterilisation since two illegitimate children were 'TWO TOO MANY', especially as my address was 'The Wagon, Peeblesshire'.

Wagon family

By the time our third child Benjamin was due, thirteen years later, in 1986, I was dreading the expected waves of judgement, but this time nobody asked if I was married or not (I wasn't), and nobody offered me adoption – or sterilisation. Robert had just been attending the birth of two Clydesdale foals and ran into the labour room to be in time for this baby, with straw in his hair. Everyone laughed. I think that was the moment I loved us best.

I am told my father fondly referred to my children as Vashti's little bastards.

The Continuing Diamond Daydream, 1970

Joe had taken the tapes away with him to the USA after the recording and so I had no say in what happened to it all after that. One day, after Leif was born, in July 1970, I received a package. It was the acetate demo of the album that would become *Just Another Diamond Day*.

Hard to describe how I felt when hearing it for the first time. It had been nine months since the Sound Techniques recording and I had detached from it. So much had changed in my life since then and I was more enchanted by this baby of mine than any music I might have ever made. My brother was upset with me as he thought my voice had not been recorded the way he would have, himself.

Having come from the Andrew Oldham days where everything was so polished, I didn't love the awkward notes that didn't need to be there and that Joe had kept in. There were many things that I couldn't bear – mostly the folky nature of it. I wouldn't have kept the fiddle on 'Jog Along Bess', I'd have had it just guitar and Christopher's perfect piano. And I didn't like the Gaelic part of 'Iris's Song For Us' because I had another version of it. Our Hebridean neighbour Wally Dix had translated the words into Gaelic for me, and found a Gaelic tune that would fit. I knew she would be upset if I didn't use it, and as we had been planning to stay living next to her – upsetting her had not been an option. But I didn't like that tune, I didn't like singing in Gaelic, and my accent was terrible.

I did like some of it – I loved 'Rose Hip November' with Robin Williamson's exquisite whistle and harp, and especially the ones that Robert Kirby arranged – but I couldn't relate to the ones that gave it that folk edge. I thought it sounded too delicate, and I couldn't really listen to it. Some of the songs are walking pace, and others hark back to the rocking comfort of childhood songs, which is maybe why it was later described as nursery rhymes. I am told it can calm fretful babies. That would be right, since I wrote a lot of the songs to calm a fretful me.

It felt to me like Joe had the idea of the album sounding like it had been recorded round a campfire – but I really did not. I didn't want it to sound handmade; it wasn't what I'd envisaged. It was as if it was his portrait of me and that when I came to see the finished work, I did not recognise myself.

However, I would never have recorded those songs at all without him and, from here, after all, I am amazed and genuinely grateful that he did keep his promise.

* * *

By the end of 1970 I'd lost the thread with music. I'd had no radio or record player for a while, and had long since stopped reading the music papers.

I had never sought the company of other musicians, but I met Nick Drake a few times in Joe's office. He was already clearly finding things very difficult and turning away to face the wall, which I found hard because I took it personally. I just thought he didn't like me, which could of course have been the way that it was. He seemed like a mysterious, slightly crumpled, black-clad and unknowable figure to me – a beautiful person, almost spectral. Then Joe had me go to Nick's house, for us to try to write a song together, which was a complete disaster because both of us were so uncommunicative. Nick was hunched over this dusty old upright piano, not saying a word, and I had a baby Leif who cried every time I picked up my guitar. Nick's shoulders went higher and higher. It was never going to work; I don't know why Joe ever thought it could, since neither of us knew the other's music. When eventually I did come to know Nick

Drake's songs I was certain that I could never, ever, have come anywhere near his genius. He knew what he was. I knew what I was not.

During my last visit to Joe's Witchseason office he gave me a few copies of *Just Another Diamond Day*, which was apparently soon to be released. Originally the cover was going to be a photograph of me, Robert, our neighbour Wally Dix, her daughter Norma with a violin, some cows and some sheep, taken in front of Ferry Cottage by Christopher Sykes – but in the end I decided that it felt too real, and didn't speak of the way we were. John James was asked to paint his own idea of us, with a photograph Christopher had taken of me at the door in my mother's pink spotty apron pasted into the middle. John's painting included a black horse which felt good because Bess had not been with us on the island for the photographs.

I loved the artwork, though John was upset that the wording he'd carefully designed to go along the roof at the top had been removed and a banner put in instead. Then because whoever Philips, the label, had working on it had not known I wanted to be Vashti Bunyan not just Vashti, 'Bunyan' was added with what looks like a Rotring pen. I was delighted with Christopher's silhouette of Bess and the wagon inside the gatefold, and very moved by Joe's words next to it. I loved the *look* of the record, but not the sound.

* * *

No one, least of all me, seemed to expect anything of the album; it had been a year from the writing of the songs to the recording, and a further year till release. I thought it had missed its small window of opportunity, that times had moved on, and that people were in general more cynical and less likely to take any notice of it. I was right.

Joe gave me the choice: stay in London and promote it with live shows, or go to stay in one of the Incredible String Band's cottages at Glen Row, in the Scottish Borders. I chose the latter – I'd grown up in London always longing for the country, I'd tried so hard to get away, and I was only back there reluctantly. I didn't want to raise my son in the city, and the offer of a roof was too good to turn down; we were homeless and staying on friends' floors again.

Glen Row was eight farmworkers' cottages, with numbers 1, 3, 5 and 7 occupied by Mike Heron, Rose Simpson, Robin Williamson and Licorice. Life there was a world of its own, warm and insular and quite unlike anything else I've known. It had an air of unreality, what with the success and comparative wealth of the String Band, and the relative struggle of ordinary folks such as us in numbers 2, 4, 6 and 8.

Bess was kindly transported in a horsebox down from North Uist by a friend of Christopher Sykes. It felt so good to have her with us again although Robin wasn't happy about the piles of horse shit on the path outside his door, which he flicked back into the grass with a stick. The wagon stayed on the island and was apparently used as a chicken shed and we were told later that the 1908 Morris Cowley wheels had been sold to a passing dealer.

The first weeks at Glen Row were good, then things changed. Scientology crept in too much for my liking. I was resistant in every way, and it made it difficult to be there. I was apparently a Potential Trouble Source which made me a bit proud.

Just Another Diamond Day finally came out at the end of 1970, although it was not listed anywhere nor advertised at all. Philips did no promotion, probably because I had refused to play any shows. I gave only one interview – in early 1971 (which I barely remember) and the only review I happened to see in a music paper said it had made the writer feel depressed. I was reading it on the path outside number 2 Glen Row and thinking, 'I've just made somebody feel unhappy. I'm not doing that again.' I remember vividly closing that paper and vowing I would not pick up a guitar again. I didn't finish the song Joe had asked me to write for Judy Collins, I gave away all my copies of the album, and I kept very little of it except the original John James painting for the sleeve.

I've said elsewhere: 'In fact it was not really released, it just edged its way out, blushed and shuffled off into oblivion.'

Like me. From then on I couldn't listen to the sound of my own voice, because it reminded me of the album that I felt had been such a failure. I did not see it in any shops, and no one ever got in touch to comment on it. It went completely unacknowledged, even by the people I was living amongst at Glen Row. I chose to forget about it, and succeeded for nearly thirty years.

The only thing that sustained my belief in our old ways throughout that time were the words Joe had written inside the sleeve.

This record is a kind of document of a pilgrimage lasting a year and a half – Vashti and Robert and Bess (the horse) and Blue (the dog) and an old green wagon fleeing London for the Outer Hebrides. Halfway there they stopped for the winter and a friend brought Vashti back to London for a short visit. She rang me: did I remember her? And of course I remembered. I had heard her three years before at a poetry reading, singing songs of delicate beauty that melted me on the spot. I had tried without success to persuade her to make a record but she had gone on to record in other contexts, all unrewarding, before she set out for the north. Vashti's songs may seem unreal to urbanised listeners but they should listen with open hearts and minds. I have never known anyone whose music is so completely a reflection of their life and spirit.

Joe Boyd, 1970

Further

Whilst at Glen Row we decided to carry on the search for a place of our own, and after meeting people who talked of farms on the west coast of Ireland going for very little, we just went. We had an old black VW Beetle, which was untaxed, uninsured and had no starter motor. Into this we crammed all the possessions that we had not sold, and set off (jump-starting down a hill) in the spring of 1971 – with Leif on my knee and the pram wheels tied onto the roof with the belief that it might keep the police from stopping us.

We wanted to keep travelling by horse and wagon. We found a bow-top wagon outside Dublin, this time with a stove in it, and we had a friend join us with another wagon – Rakis, who'd been in the mime troupe Stone Monkey, an offshoot of the Incredible String Band.

Bess was brought over by two friends, Lindsay Cook and Lizzie McDougall, who hitchhiked with her, given lifts in cattle trucks, even across the sea. I often think of this part of those days as very telling of the way we all were, the trust we had that all would be fine. Or maybe it was just that we really didn't think things through enough to alarm ourselves with the possibility that anything might go wrong. Lindsay and Lizzie had no idea where to find us – we could have been anywhere in or around Dublin, we had no means of communication once they had left Peeblesshire in the Borders of Scotland.

Robert, Rakis, Leif and I were in our old VW having come from a visit to a Travellers' camp where we had been looking for a horse for Rakis, and there they were, two very recognisable young women standing at a bus stop just outside Dublin. I don't remember even thinking anything of it. It just was. They had found a stable to look after Bess whilst they went searching for us, so we all went to collect her and take her to our new wagons.

Rakis bought a young draught horse called Rosie, having been persuaded that she was well used to pulling carts, with her long legs and big feet. Over time we realised she had probably never even been in harness before and was in fact a Clydesdale, as she grew – and kept growing. She had been a youngster, but she pulled our wagon like an old hand, born to it, as we all set out on our way – with Bess taking Rakis's wagon as it was smaller.

* * *

Halfway across Ireland we went to visit Donovan, who by now was living in a castle. We were going to ask him to help us buy another horse as we thought Bess might be struggling. However, it turned out that he had never received the postal order for £100 that my uncle had addressed to him at Seagull's Rest in the late summer of 1968. It was the promised repayment of the original loan for Bess and the wagon, after my inheritance had come through. Someone must have cashed it but Donovan had no way of knowing that it had ever been sent. He consulted with his wife Linda who seemingly said no, as he came out to us with some pieces of chicken wrapped in silver foil, and an orange. He said that this time he couldn't help.

I still owe him £100.

We kept on walking across Ireland, but by the time we got to the west the property prices had gone up way beyond our reach – a farm would have been £600 or more. That kept happening. We stayed a year, had many adventures, so many stories to tell another time maybe, but then walked the horses and wagons back to Scotland, where I had our second baby, Whyn.

We rented a tiny flat in the old coach yard of Cromlix Estate, near Dunblane, and were taught by two Traveller sisters the art of 'knocking' the farms, buying old furniture out of barns to restore and sell on. We had a street-market stall in St Andrews, Fife, for three days a week, driving an ancient sludge-green ex-post office Commer van with Leif sitting between us on the engine cover, and Whyn on my knee, 120 miles there and back. We sold old stuff from the farms, pots and smoothing irons, butter churns and lace pillowcases, and over one summer saved up enough to buy a new white Volvo estate car. There was a house we could have bought for the same at that time, but we had learned from the Travellers that a good vehicle is the most important thing to have – and it has to be the best.

When Iris Macfarlane saw the car she cried, 'How the mighty are fallen,' but at least I knew that the Romanies understood about the joy of shiny new things in a hostile world.

After another decade living in rented houses, we eventually found the elusive place of our own. My father's courteous way with his bank manager in Deal, Kent, persuaded her to consider a loan for us so that we could buy the very old cottage and falling-down farm buildings we'd found near Gartmore, in Scotland. He doffed his old woolly hat, bowed, called her ma'am and kissed her hand. She melted, and lent us the money. We had huge interest to pay on her loan at that time, but we didn't care since we now had a place at last to restore and rebuild, a living to be made by buying, repairing and selling on old farm furniture, and a hill for the horses.

I remember in the first days, Rosie the Clydesdale scratching her backside on a little hazel tree and breaking off a branch. I gasped, 'Oh no,' until I realised – it was ours.

There we lived out some of the old ideas – but with a lot more horses, dogs, transient friends and a late, third child, Benjamin.

Black Bess had stayed with us for a number of years, out on Cromlix hill with our other horses, free at last, not even a collar. She was much older than we'd been told when we found her, and her passing whilst there left us bereft, and sad that she never did make it to our own piece of hill.

My Blue dog, with one ear up and the other ear down, lived till he was fifteen, surviving many accidents, recovering against all odds and many vets' dire predictions. He faded away gracefully in the end, in an old armchair.

It is said that you only have one dog in your life, even if you have had many others before and since. He was it for me.

Dad

After Mum died in 1969, my father went to stay much more often in the United States. He had always wanted to live there but he had never managed to persuade his wife to leave her mother. He left his hated dental surgery in London, moved the laboratory to his house in Walmer, Kent, and carried on with his experimenting and innovating. He had invented non-stick wound dressings, and a hydraulic hospital bed that would sit a patient up – with a removable part of the mattress where a bedpan could slide in – thereby saving the backs of nurses trying to lift heavy people, like him. He spent the rest of his life researching the wound-healing properties of sodium hypochlorite, trying to persuade the medical profession of his findings, but he did not have the right letters after his name.

In America he was known as Professor Bunyan – something he never achieved in the UK. They loved him over there, understood and believed in him.

So did I. I loved his mother-of-invention ways. He would bring back fancy kitchen and other gadgets from the USA, of a different voltage to the UK, and so the house was a mess of cables and transformers, matchsticks holding wires into electrical sockets where he had run out of plugs, and silver-foil sweet wrappers in place of blown fuses when he could not remember where he had put the fusewire.

He also brought back an electric typewriter for his lovingly loyal secretary – who sat typing up his notes in her rubber boots, terrified she might be electrocuted. With reason.

He wanted to rearrange his kitchen, which meant moving the gas fridge. He turned off the gas, cut the pipe and extended it with a long stretch of hose to the new position for the fridge, and joined it all up with Jubilee clips. Whilst he was away his secretary came in and smelled gas so she phoned the gas board. Horrified, they told her he could have blown up the whole street, but when she told them whose house it was they just sighed, 'Ah, Mr Bunyan,' and re-laid the pipes for him.

He had never spoken to Robert in all our years, even after Leif and Whyn were born. If ever we were with him he would address 'the boy' through me, never looking at him. However, once we had our shiny new Volvo estate car we drove down to visit him, and as we turned in through the gate, stopped and got out, he leant over the bonnet, offered his hand and said, 'Hello dear boy.' Luckily Robert came to appreciate him too, and over time we helped add to his beautiful collection of old microscopes. He was president of the Royal Microscopical Society for a while, which always made me smile as he was so much larger than life himself.

He came to visit us in Scotland, in 1981, and took us out to dinner with an American friend of his who, he said, was the first single woman to be allowed to officially adopt a child. Robert and I had dressed, as we thought, appropriately – I wore a frock and Robert a shirt and tie. That wonderful woman looked around the table and said, 'Oh my – where have all the rebels gone?'

In this demure Perthshire restaurant my stout, white-haired father – with his newly laundered shirt, slightly dinner-stained, ash-dusted tie and bright red braces – leapt from his chair and shouted '*I'M* still a rebel, they'll never get *ME*.'

They never did get him. His secretary told me that he had managed to keep the inland revenue off his back for years by getting her to write endless letters, but he thought the end of the road had come one day when he looked out of an upstairs window onto the hats of two trench-coated men. He had a massive stroke, was never able to speak again and died soon after, in December 1983.

When my brother, sister and I were clearing his house and dividing things between us, we brought down a big old ugly vase from the top of a bookcase. Inside was a note – 'This is for Vashti if no one else wants it.' It still makes me laugh.

At one time he had put into his will that it would be up to my sister to decide if I should be given anything or not. He apparently changed it as he and I became closer later in his life. In all of it, every clip round the ear, every cruel joke at my expense, I never really felt unloved. It was just his way. And mine.

John Bunyan in his lab

Unbound

My father told me many times when I was young that he couldn't think why anyone would want to marry me. He thought it was funny and I expect I laughed too.

There were no dreams of lacy white weddings for me. It just didn't enter my head – maybe it had never been able to – but watching some of my young female friends marry and become chained and controlled and miserable made me quite sure I could not do that, would not be that.

So, now, how about this for a way to be – believing that people did not belong to people, and that loving is to set them free? If I love, I will want that person to be happy, won't I? Even if it is with someone else. I don't love so as to be loved, I love to love. I wonder who told me that.

The idea was to be generous and open-hearted enough to let a lover be anywhere and with whomever they wanted, and so I tried not to be hurt, to hold on to that belief and not let caustic jealousy overwhelm my days. There was never any dishonesty, nothing hidden, but that didn't make it any easier.

I didn't do so well as I mostly felt silent resentment where love should have been, and guilty fury where generosity should have been. Apart from one. I always loved her.

Somehow, I instinctively understood that only one of us, in the kind of couple that Robert and I were, could be the one to have other people. If both of us were faithless I feared that we would break apart completely.

And so it was – after twenty whole years – that I fell and loved another, and I had to choose between my new blue-eyed love and my long-time love, whose blue eyes were now light green with pain.

A bar in Glasgow – black and white marble-tiled floor, palm-like plants in Grecian urns, heart-tearing music. I was sitting at a table, old love brought me flowers. He never had before.

How to describe the splitting feeling. My soul torn in two – no, not that, but my whole being. The black or white tiles. There was no grey way. Who to inflict pain on the most. How could I break the home, the children and the long-established ways? I would have to choose to stay – and to hurt instead and send away, forever, (and it was forever), the one I had almost allowed into the fortress I had always built.

I stayed, lost and resentful, locked in grief.

And so – two years later – old love left.

The end, for good this time, of all those diamond days.

The Leaving

Living the way we did in those early days of the Bess journey there was no going back – and we did carry on. It was not as if we could return from our little old wagon adventure and take up where we left off. There was nothing to take up.

We made our own lives, *Lived on wit, got away with it*, and we managed to be more or less with each other and have three children. But yes, after twenty-two years of us, Robert left for good, for London and a whole different way of life within a world of famous actors, the world he had perhaps always wanted.

The diamond daydream went away with him. Leif soon left for California, Whyn for Glasgow School of Art, and I stayed on our farm with Benjamin, dogs, horses and the workshop cat. The workshop cabinet makers stayed with me too, and we carried on making, restoring, trading.

On the hill above the farmhouse there was a mysterious lone lump of rock, white quartz, as big as an upturned boat – deposited after the last ice age – and sometimes, before Robert left, I would go up and stand on the very top of it and yell at the sky rather than be done for homicide. Years of dogged domesticity, of one kind and another, sinks and suds, scrubbing brushes and muddy floors, *days going by in clouds of flour and white washing* – there had to be more than this. Living out in the hills brings a different kind of crazy to the city kind, and it took me a while to decide which I could do the best.

Two years after Robert left, the farm was sold, and the workshop closed down. I rehomed the horses and, with sadness, my bees. Whyn, Ben, dogs and I moved to the city. We slowly made a new stitched-together family with Al Campbell and his three children, Rowan, Rachel and

Patrick, who would neatly fit into the thirteen-year gap between my Whyn and Benjamin, all of them, with mine, managing these uncharted waters of a stepfamily with grace and good nature. I love them, easily and dearly.

And Al, oh so faithfully.

I open my eyes
And you are there
With no surprise
No pain to bear
I scan the horizon
For clouds to appear
I close my eyes
And you are here

'Here', *Heartleap*, 2012

For me it was a little like going home, as the place we moved to was very similar to where I had grown up in London, but the dogs were not happy at first, having had untold freedom all of their lives, and I had to get used to chimneypot skylines again, instead of my untidy lime trees against the sky. I did miss the warmth of the bran mash for the horses on a winter's morning, the peaty smoke from an open fire and the big skies all around me, but now I would not go back.

The hill behind the old house,
I can trace it with my finger,
Against the sky I see it still,
And draw it down on paper.

'Against the Sky', *Lookaftering*, 2004

Tech

Al and I have six children between us. In varying combinations our house was teeming, streaming with ins and outs, ups and downs. I walked up and down the hall one day when everyone was out and wondered, 'What am I, what *AM* I?' I avoided parties where people asked me what I did – and my answer was 'nothing'. Building shelves and scrubbing stairs would not have counted as something in this new city world I had come to.

In 1997 I got onto the internet for the first time. Typing my name into a search engine brought up a few surprises. A vinyl collector in Sacramento called Don Stout had posted on an Incredible String Band site, asking if anyone knew what had happened to me. I wrote to him and he let me know that *Just Another Diamond Day* was selling for surprising amounts on the collectors' market because of its rarity, and that the soundtrack of *Tonite Let's All Make Love in London* was out on CD and included 'Winter Is Blue'. Most pleasing of all was finding 'I'd Like to Walk Around in Your Mind', which I hadn't heard for nearly thirty years. In 1969 Iris Macfarlane on Uist had liked the song when I played it to her, so I gave her my acetate demo as a thank you. Somehow it had worked its way into the collection of Phil Smee, who included it on an album called *Circus Days: Pop-Sike Obscurities* in 1990. I had known nothing about it, being blissfully unaware of any music of mine being out in the world at all. I thought it was all forever forgotten and disappeared.

I had long been used to that disappearance, but it set me on the path to finding out who my old recordings belonged to – and brought me in contact with Paul Lambden, who was then working at Rykomusic. He'd found the old publishing contracts for *Just Another Diamond Day* and was curious to know how the songs sounded. I knew someone who had a vinyl album and asked him to tape a copy for me, which I sent to Paul. He called me and said, 'I like it.'

I like it.

That was the first time I had ever heard those words. He said it should come out again, so we set about trying to find who owned the master, which took a long, long time and there were many moments when I came close to giving up. We eventually traced the master tape to where it had lain in a warehouse for thirty years. I collected it but made the mistake of travelling with it in a thunderstorm and took it on an underground train with it sitting in my bag on the floor – both of which could have wiped it, I was told afterwards.

I found a way to get the rights back. I'd only ever heard it on old record players or tapes that had been taped from scratchy vinyl, so when Paul and I took the original to be remastered, that was the first time I'd listened to it through big speakers, and realised, 'Ah! This is what Joe did.' I had never been able to hear how well he had produced it, always just feeling it was not really mine. I had not been able to listen to it at all for years and years without a confused kind of sadness.

I did not sing to my children and would never let them hear the old album, or know anything much about it, but my daughter tells me that she and her brother once found an old dusty tape copy in the back of a drawer. I had hidden it. They took it out to the car to play it – secretly.

During the remastering we took out some of the awkward notes that had always upset me, and tightened up the lagging between the verses of 'Rainbow River'. I wasn't sure about Robert Kirby's trumpet on the end of 'Timothy Grub' but Paul said it was one of the things he loved best about it. Maybe that was the turning point for me, and from then on I didn't have to cover my ears any more.

Paul formed the label Spinney for the reissue in July, 2000. We added four bonus tracks, partly to illustrate Joe's description of the first songs he'd heard me sing at that poetry reading in 1966, and then my brother's recording of Iris's song, the version I hadn't used for the original album. I so wished that I had asked Robert Kirby to write an arrangement for it, instead of recording the Gaelic version.

I expected a rerun of the old dismissal of it as lightweight songs for children and I was all ready to hide away again forever, but this time it was so, so different. There was a four-star review in the *Guardian* that I was able to read to my brother just before he died. It felt as if many of the reviews were saying all that I could ever have wished for back when the album emerged, it seemed that the world had become a little bit kinder, with a new generation of people unafraid to listen more closely.

I myself listened to it again with different ears, trying to hear it as it might sound thirty and more years on to people who were not around when the album was made – when it was possible to live as I lived, to have those sixties dreams and to be able to make them real. Maybe it doesn't seem so possible now.

However, at the time I was writing the songs I wasn't just living in the freedom of the hills and highways and the beautiful world around me, I was living in my head and trying to make sense of the tumbleweed within it. I have been told that the album has in these days helped a few people with their own tumbled minds. So different to the reviewer in 1971 who said he had been made depressed by the album. That review had me stop completely. The new ones had me start again, start writing and recording again.

I didn't expect those songs to be heard when I was writing them, so it's quite unselfconsciously a document of its time. Now it's far enough away, I can forgive it – for being unlike anything else. More than that, I'm proud of our life on that road – having almost nothing, making it up as we went along, attempting to change our lives and to put different meaning into them.

That it resulted in some wonderful progeny was always the best thing for me. Robert had said, in an interview when asked what we were going to do once we had reached the end of our horse-drawn journey, that we would 'breed horses and dogs – and people'. We did that.

Ferry, Berneray

Another art-school friend of Robert's, Chris Spears, had taken on the roofless byre down on the shore by Ferry Cottage, after we'd left Berneray in 1970. He built it up, made a home, made a life there – all that Robert and I might have done had we stayed. Chris eventually managed to overcome all the feudal problems and get ownership of his house and later the ruin of Ferry Cottage, which was wonderful to know. Just recently he visited and as he came into the kitchen he told me he thought I should sit down.

'I've demolished Ferry,' he said. It was too far gone to restore to its old self, impossible to put a roof on such broken walls. He was going to use the stones for a new building, a bunkhouse for visitors to the island. So life moves on, as it should. I did cry, but only after he had gone.

Thinking of Ferry, I remember, from the days after *Just Another Diamond Day* was reissued in 2000, I was approached by two young people in a London café. They told me how much they loved the album and that they were going on a pilgrimage to the Outer Hebrides to look for the house with the animals painted on the outside. It was so hard having to tell them that no, the album cover was from a painting by John James, and that the animals were not painted onto the house walls. I hated that they were so crestfallen.

Now the house itself is gone, but I have John's painting, and that will be with me always.

Onward

Drawing was my first real love. In my early days at school, five years old, I drew a perfect square. I showed it to the child sitting next to me and said, 'Look – a perfect square!' and the cry went up around the table – 'Boaster!' So that must have gone in deep. If in 1970 I had taken my recording of 'Diamond Day' and said, 'Look – a perfect song!' someone might have listened, but I was still set in my way of waiting for someone else to say it first. They didn't. I waited for thirty years. Well, no, I wasn't waiting, I had no idea it might ever happen.

Since Paul's Spinney reissue in 2000, *Just Another Diamond Day* has had a second life, and given me another life too. I picked up my guitar and it no longer gave me the sounds of failure and sadness. When I'm asked now what I do I no longer have to say 'nothing'.

With the first royalties from Paul I bought a Mac, a small mixer and some music software. The first attempts belong at the bottom of the sea.

Devendra Banhart sent me some songs and some drawings and I recognised them, and him, immediately. Some people you just know from the start, and he has been the truest of friends ever since. He later sent me a song he had recorded and wanted me to add something to. To be able to record at home and send it over to the USA and have it appear on his album was a magical thing for me. Devendra also introduced me to his friend Gary Held who licensed *Just Another Diamond Day* from Paul for the USA, releasing it on his Dicristina label, after Michael Gira decided for, and then against, taking it on.

Email brought me back in contact with Andrew Loog Oldham, through a mutual acquaintance. It had been a very long time since we had last seen or heard of each other – he said he had been thirty years 'out to lunch' and I said I had been thirty years up farm tracks. He has shown me much kindness and wisdom over the years since. Advice, too. Stay close to, and look after, your hearth.

Love Songs

It became time to think about returning to the kind of songs and music that I made before 'Diamond Day'. The kind I left behind after Robert Lewis's 'Why don't you stop writing those miserable little love songs?'

Same, but different.

I'm in a boat
On the sea
And I see
You on the shore
So sure
Of yourself

You're in a boat
On the sea
And you see
Me on the shore
So sure
Of myself

We're in a boat
All at sea
And we see
We are the same
The same
But different

'Same But Different', *Lookaftering*, 2003

203

* * *

I had a call from Paul Lambden to say that Glen Johnson of Piano Magic had written a song he'd like me to sing for their next album. I went to London, walked into a studio for the first time since recording *Just Another Diamond Day* thirty-four years before, and stood in front of a microphone and wondered nervously if any sound might come out of my mouth. I sang 'Crown of the Lost', astonished myself that I still had a voice, walked back out into the London streets and called my daughter to tell her I wanted to record again, make an album, try it all over again, take the risk again. It's true about walking on air.

Then there was a bolt from the blue when Stephen Malkmus was curating a show at the Royal Festival Hall in London and invited me to sing three songs. I had met Simon Raymonde whilst recording for Piano Magic as he played keyboard on the song, and he agreed to accompany me at the Festival Hall. Then he said, 'Oh dear, no, I forgot – I have to be in Barcelona that day . . . but I have a couple of friends who might help – Kieran Hebden and Adem.'

I had not performed live for over thirty years, and even back then very rarely. We played three songs, with another friend of Simon's – Fiona Brice, on violin. How great they all were to stand behind me, to push me and make me do it. I shook with fear through the whole performance, but it was a start, a toe in the water, a foot on the stage.

* * *

Kieran was soon playing a show in Edinburgh as Fourtet, with Animal Collective as his support, and we all had dinner together. So shy, all of them, from the USA.

Kieran said, 'These guys all have your record.' I said, 'Why?' So bad-mannered. What I really meant was how on earth could that happen – with them being all the way from over there? But I later heard they wanted to record three songs with me, and so again I went to London. That was an unforgettable three days, one song a day, not backing vocals as I'd thought but out in front, with them having me singing like I didn't know I could. Dave Portner wanted to record his vocal in the echoey bathroom of the studio and so the engineer took a lead all the way there and back for him. It sounded so good. It was for the FatCat label, and so there I met Dave Howell. He was busy going all over London trying to source a particular mic that they needed and I was impressed by his care for them.

We got talking and he asked me what I was doing. I told him I was writing songs again and so he asked to hear them. My home recordings wended their way to Dave and to my great surprise and happiness he offered me a deal with FatCat, and an introduction to Max Richter, the composer, who lived near to me in Edinburgh at the time.

* * *

My second album was released by FatCat in 2005, thirty-five years after my first. Max Richter was a sympathetic, engaging, fun and inspiring producer. After every vocal take he would say, 'That's *such* a good song, ah – let's do it one more time.' He made me laugh and I felt quite all right. Thank you, Max.

Then there were the generous contributions from other musicians. Joanna Newsom, tiny in an empty Glasgow studio with an enormous harp and broken fingertips fixed up with superglue after a hard tour. Then we had one day booked in a London studio, with Adem and his suitcase on wheels filled with every instrument we might ever have needed, Devendra Banhart (my most faithful of all advocates), Otto Hauser and Andy Cabic and Kevin Barker of the USA band Vetiver, classical string-playing friends of Max, and a beautiful girl who came into the studio to play cor anglais and then disappeared as quietly as she had appeared.

And Robert Kirby, on that same day. I hadn't seen him since he had arranged three of the songs on *Just Another Diamond Day* but he agreed to play trumpet and French horn on two of the new tracks. So, all those years later I was able to apologise to him for the way I had behaved back then – but he laughed. It was so very good to see him.

He said, 'We're the survivors' – with his eyes brimming. I did know what he meant.

The mastering day was a revelation. Meeting engineer Mandy Parnell, nervous that she might not like the recordings, but it seemed that she did. At the end she turned to me to ask what the album was to be called. I had thought about calling it *Dead Pets* – as in measuring my life in them – but the only person there who liked that was Kieran Evans, who made the film *From Here to Before*, his documentary about my horse and wagon journey. He understood.

But during the mastering I had realised that the songs were a lot about looking back, where my first album had been so much about looking forward. In the dead pets silence I mentioned that there was a word my family had come up with, lookaftering, meaning to care for someone or something. It could just as well apply to these songs about looking back – I said – and was surprised when everyone there shouted, 'Yes that's it!'

So *Lookaftering* it became.

* * *

After the release, interviewers were sometimes surprised that I turned up with no horse, with no long dress nor apron, no purple velvet, no beads in my hair – but dressed in jeans and a T-shirt. I had to remind them that it had been thirty-five years between albums. When asked what I had been doing in all that time I could only answer, 'I lived a life.'

I then started to say yes to everything, even touring.

The musicians who joined me as my band were much younger than me, but they understood the songs so well, and we played in places I could never have imagined. First of all head-lining a Barbican show in London, with Joe Boyd introducing us. I was accompanied by the guitarist Gareth Dickson, when neither of us had done anything like it in all of our lives, only meeting, rehearsing and playing the songs for just one month before the show. We have played everywhere together ever since.

From Carnegie Hall in New York at the invitation of David Byrne, to a tin shed on the Yorkshire moors, from tiny churches to enormous halls. The USA, Australia, Canada, Russia, Singapore, Japan and all over Europe.

And yes, I said yes to a request from T-Mobile in 2006 to use the song 'Diamond Day' for a new commercial. Whilst driving down the Taconic State Parkway to New York City from my sister's house in Staatsburg, my phone rang. It was Paul Lambden, telling me that T-Mobile had agreed the deal. I remember saying to Paul that nothing would ever be the same again. He said he knew, and it wasn't.

I did upset a lot of people by saying yes though, those who loved the song for its seemingly anti-commercial stance. My response was to say that I had always been told in my young days that my songs were 'uncommercial, dear', and so this was a kind of validation, a deeply, darkly, wonderfully unexpected thing to happen – and I loved it.

Robert Kirby said not to worry about it, that music is meant to be heard, not hidden away.

———

'A Suitcase Full of Notes'

from 'Wayward', *Lookaftering*, 2004

When moving away from my brother's house in 1970, after Leif was born, I left an old suitcase in one of the sheds. Inside were the newspaper cuttings that my mother had faithfully kept, photographs, some acetate demos and the scores for all the many individual instruments that David Whitaker had arranged for the single 'Some Things Just Stick in Your Mind'. A year later my brother was moving house and asked me if I wanted the suitcase. I said no as I was walking across Ireland with two wagons, two horses, two travelling companions, two dogs, a year-old baby, three chickens and a cat at the time, and anyway had no desire to have anything more to do with my musical past. He left it in the shed. Five years later he bought that house back again, with the suitcase still there in the same place in the same shed.

This time I did take it away, opened it and firmly shut it again. It came with me through several moves and travels over the years but I always looked at it with a bit of a shudder. It stayed in dripping lofts and damp barns, looking sadder and sadder, until I did eventually open it. All the edges of the papers and photographs were pink and green and black, and the acetate demos were green with mould, but David Whitaker's scores for 'Some Things Just Stick in Your Mind' had survived intact.

Oxford's latest pop singer

Vashi is 20. She was thrown out of the Ruskin 12 months ago. Now she has made a record — produced by Andrew Oldham. Title : "Some Things Just Stick in Your Mind." At Oxford she sang with the Fourbeats and was a close friend of humourist Robert Hewison. "Some Things" was written by Rolling Stones Mick Jagger and Keith Richard. She composed the flip side.

In 2007 Paul Lambden, and Dave Howell at FatCat, along with Gary Held of Dicristina, decided to put together a CD of my early singles and demos from the time before *Just Another Diamond Day*, and some recordings that my brother had made in those days, and had put onto cassette tapes for me just before he died.

I also had a box that he had sent me years before of some quarter-inch tapes he'd found in his attic. I didn't have anything to play them on then, but later when I had borrowed a reel-to-reel machine I brought them out from the back of a cupboard. The biggest shock was finding that he had kept safely the recording I'd made in a studio when returning from New York in 1964. Those twelve tracks, with me announcing each title as I went, brought my oh-so-young and English self into the present, with some songs I had forgotten completely.

I have likened it to finding teenage poetry in the back of a drawer, but still, Dave Howell and Mandy Parnell and I took the old tape to be converted to digital. The reel-to-reel player there was old and slightly wobbly but it didn't seem to matter as the decision was made to have a double CD and double vinyl of all the early singles and demos, with that first, unedited recording on disc two.

We called it *Some Things Just Stick in Your Mind: Singles and Demos 1964–1967*. For the cover we used a photograph taken by Robert Hewison in 1966. I would like to be able to lie and say that the coat was fake fur but no, it wasn't. So very sorry, rabbits, I should have known better.

The package, with photographs and newspaper cuttings

from the old suitcase, is out of print now in its original form, but I'm grateful that Paul Lambden, FatCat and Gary Held put that collection together when they did. I wanted it to show that I was never a folk singer – maybe it worked or maybe it didn't, but I hope it helped.

* * *

By 2009 Robert Kirby and I were planning to work together on some new songs. He had so many ideas, and had just been recording with an orchestra who had a tuba player he thought he might invite. Perfect.

And then came the phone call, his wife telling me, 'The Maestro has died.' And so now, I have sadly survived him, dear, funny, irreverent and lovely man.

After a while of devastated loss, I decided that no one could replace him and so I had to carry on – on my own.

I had learned so much from Max Richter, by watching him record and edit in his home studio, so I had applied to a local college to be on a music software course. I wanted to get to grips myself with that screen, the representation of all the faders and knobs and lights that had been so fascinating and forbidden to a young singer in a sixties studio.

The college said I was too old and wouldn't be able to understand it. A bit like that biker in Oxford who would not teach me how to play 'Blowin' in the Wind' because he said a girl shouldn't be singing a Dylan song. So, again, I taught myself.

Nine years after *Lookaftering*, 2014's *Heartleap* was completed, and released by FatCat. Written, recorded, edited, produced, arranged and mostly played by me. I had time. I realised that I liked working alone, to know that no one could overhear me, to be able to make horrible mistakes and keep them hidden, to only allow people to hear what I was happy with.

I wanted to learn, to find out, to be completely selfish and shut myself away – and so I did – especially for the last months. My partner Al came into my studio room with a cup of tea one day, and stood in front of my desk for ten minutes before I even saw that he was there.

I remembered Andrew Oldham's words – to 'stay close to, and look after, your hearth', and I will never move so far from it again.

Heartleap was mastered by Mandy Parnell as before with *Lookaftering*. At the end she turned to me and asked when I would be recording the next one as she would like to come and rearrange my studio for me, make it work better. I gasped. 'No – I'm never doing this again!'

And so it was said in the press release that this would be my last album.

Road Without End

Thinking back over all the songs that I have ever written and the albums that I made, *Just Another Diamond Day* just did not feel anything like mine in the end and so I left it, and music, out of my life altogether. I abandoned it, but now I feel as if I have found a child after missing all its years of growing up. Or maybe it found me. I see it, hear it and even quite love it.

Lookaftering was an awakening – leading to endless possibilities, taking me to another life and, oh, such a different kind of road. A road I shared with Al.

The *Some Things . . .* double album of old singles and demos, allowed that young person out again, the one who had tried to be heard with a small voice in the loud gale of the sixties.

Heartleap, almost fifty years after my first ever recordings, was my chance to say what I had always wanted to say, and to sound the way I had always wanted to sound. But recordings will still be put through many processes before reaching their intended audience in quite the same shape as was imagined in their beginnings. This is maybe why I like demos as much as I do.

So, now I think about my daughter Whyn, the painter. Surely hers would be the better way. A painting would not go out into the world and then be altered, or changed to earthly colours when it had started out sky blue.

Maybe I should have paid more attention at the Ruskin School of Drawing and Fine Art, but then, *all I ever wanted was a road without end.*

Wayward

Didn't want to be the one
The one who's left behind
While the other one goes out to life
And comes back home to find
Me, sitting pretty happily
Surrounded by a house
With cups in all their saucers
And not a bit of dust
Days going by in clouds
Of flour and white washing
Life getting lost in a world
Without end

I wanted to be the one
With road dust on my boots
And a single silver earring
And a suitcase full of notes

WAYWARD

And a band of wayward children
With their fathers left behind
All in their castles in their air
And houses in their land
Lives getting lost in mending gaps
In their fencing
All I ever wanted was a road
Without end

'Wayward', *Lookaftering*, 2004

Acknowledgements

Thank you . . .

Kieran Evans for introducing me to Lee Brackstone at White Rabbit.

Lee Brackstone for guiding me through uncharted waters.

Ellie Freedman at White Rabbit too, for help and understanding.

Lisa Baker for all the calming.

Martha Sprackland, and especially Rosie Pearce at Orion, for dealing with all my changes.

Chevonne Elbourne for the cover design.

All have been patient and encouraging, even when I was not.

Jenny Lewis for Oxford days.

Alastair Clayre for 'Train Song'.

Robert Lewis for the journey and diamond years.

John James for being there, and Rose, his mother.

Donovan for Bess, and the dream of Skye.

Christopher Simon Sykes, Anthony McCall and Robert Hewison for their photographs, taken so long ago but still luminous.

Mac and Iris Macfarlane for the wintering.

ACKNOWLEDGEMENTS

Doon Granville for the oranges.
Wally Dix and Gealachas for the milk.

Joe Boyd for keeping his promise.
Andrew Loog Oldham for keeping me going.
Paul Lambden for the '*I like it*' – and making Spinney for JADD.
Glen Johnson for finding my voice.
Max Richter for making the *Lookaftering* days magical.
Dave Howell and Alex Knight at FatCat Records, Gary Held at Dicristina in USA, for their faith in me.
Dave Thomas (DLT) for the record sleeve designs.
Devendra Banhart for spreading the words.
Adem for his suitcase full of notes.
My UK band – Fiona Brice, Jo Mango, Gareth Dickson, Emma Smith and Ian Burdge.
And in USA – Kevin Barker, Katt Hernandez and Helena Espvall.
Howard Wuelfing, Todd Cote and Zach Cowie.

Richard Lewis for his permission to use five-year-old Hilary Ann Farley's poem 'I Love Animals and Dogs'.
Alfie Ball for 'horse, van and harness'.
Black Bess, Wayward Magog and Blue, and all others since.

My beautiful mother, and my father who adored her.
Brother John, so very missed.
Sister-in-law Inda for all the mothering.

Sister Sue for love and wisdom, and her wife, Hilary, for all the Staatsburg sun.

My children, my dears, Leif, Whyn and Benjamin Lewis. They always wanted me to tell them more of the story, so I'm hoping this will shine some light. I am forever sorry for never singing to them when they were little.

Rowan, Rachel Almeida and Patrick Campbell, my dear steps. Their mother Lesley was the only one I knew who listened to and sang 'Rainbow River' when no one else did. She sang it to them and now Rachel sings it to her Noah, and Rowan to her Naomi.

My grandsons Riley Wagner Lewis, Cal Lewis Hall, Noah Campbell Almeida, and my granddaughter Naomi Campbell Swan.

Katie Wagner Lewis, Iain Swan, Nuno Almeida, Aline Mokfa and Larissa Hadlum.

Lindsay Cook and Toby Cook, Jenny Richardson, Corrina Seddon and Mike Heron, Lizzie McDougall, John Oliphant.

And always, Al Campbell for being ever kind, for look-aftering all of us, and showing me a world that I never knew before. Also for his great help with this story. Thankyou is not a big enough word, my evermore love.

Text Credits

'I Don't Know What Love Is' written by Vashti Bunyan, 1963. Branch Music Ltd.

'Some Things Just Stick in Your Mind' written by Mick Jagger & Keith Richards © 1964 ABKCO Music, Inc. Reprinted by permission. All rights reserved.

'I'd Like to Walk Around in Your Mind' written by Vashti Bunyan, 1966. Branch Music Ltd.

'Winter Is Blue' written by Vashti Bunyan, 1966. Branch Music Ltd.

'Across the Water' written by Vashti Bunyan, 2010. Branch Music Ltd.

'Glow Worms' written by Vashti Bunyan, 1968. BMG Rights Management (UK) Ltd.

'I Love Animals and Dogs' by Hilary-Anne Farley, age 5, is from *Miracles: Poems by Children of the English-speaking World*, collected by Richard Lewis, originally published by Simon and Schuster, 1966 © Richard Lewis, 1966.

'Timothy Grub' written by Vashti Bunyan, 1968. BMG Rights Management (UK) Ltd.

'Rainbow River' written by Vashti Bunyan, 1968. BMG Rights Management (UK) Ltd.

'Diamond Day' written by Vashti Bunyan, 1968. BMG Rights Management (UK) Ltd.

'Mother' written by Vashti Bunyan, 2011. Branch Music Ltd.

'Come Wind Come Rain' written by Vashti Bunyan, 1969. BMG Rights Management (UK) Ltd.

'Here' written by Vashti Bunyan, 2012. Branch Music Ltd.

'Against the Sky' written by Vashti Bunyan, 2004. Branch Music Ltd.

'Same but Different' written by Vashti Bunyan, 2003. Branch Music Ltd.

'Wayward' written by Vashti Bunyan, 2004. Branch Music Ltd.

(With thanks to BMG, ABKCO and Branch Music.)

List of Illustrations

All drawings by Vashti Bunyan, between 1986 and 2021.

LIST OF ILLUSTRATIONS

LIST OF ILLUSTRATIONS